OPPOSING
VIEWPOINTS®
SERIES

Universal Health Care

Other Books of Related Interest:

Opposing Viewpoints Series

Alternative Medicine

The Pharmaceutical Industry

Resurgent Diseases

At Issue Series

Do Infectious Diseases Pose a Threat?

Cancer

Current Controversies Series

Alternative Therapies

Vaccines

"Congress shall make no law . . . abridging the freedom of speech, or of the press."

First Amendment to the U.S. Constitution

The basic foundation of our democracy is the First Amendment guarantee of freedom of expression. The *Opposing Viewpoints* series is dedicated to the concept of this basic freedom and the idea that it is more important to practice it than to enshrine it.

Universal Health Care

Susan Hunnicutt, Book Editor

GREENHAVEN PRESS
A part of Gale, Cengage Learning

Detroit • New York • San Francisco • New Haven, Conn • Waterville, Maine • London

Christine Nasso, *Publisher*
Elizabeth Des Chenes, *Managing Editor*

© 2010 Greenhaven Press, a part of Gale, Cengage Learning

Gale and Greenhaven Press are registered trademarks used herein under license.

For more information, contact:
Greenhaven Press
27500 Drake Rd.
Farmington Hills, MI 48331-3535
Or you can visit our Internet site at gale.cengage.com

For product information and technology assistance, contact us at

Gale Customer Support, 1-800-877-4253
For permission to use material from this text or product, submit all requests online at
www.cengage.com/permissions

Further permissions questions can be emailed to permissionrequest@cengage.com

Articles in Greenhaven Press anthologies are often edited for length to meet page require-ments. In addition, original titles of these works are changed to clearly present the main thesis and to explicitly indicate the author's opinion. Every effort is made to ensure that Greenhaven Press accurately reflects the original intent of the authors. Every effort has been made to trace the owners of copyrighted material.

Cover image copyright IBI, 2009. Used under license from shutterstock.com.

LIBRARY OF CONGRESS CATALOGING-IN-PUBLICATION DATA

Universal health care / Susan Hunnicutt, book editor.
        p. cm. -- (Opposing viewpoints)
    Includes bibliographical references and index.
    ISBN 978-0-7377-4648-8 (hardcover) -- ISBN 978-0-7377-4649-5 (pbk.)
    1. National health insurance--United States--Popular works. 2. Medical care--United States--Popular works. 3. Health services accessibility--United States--Popular works. I. Hunnicutt, Susan.
    RA412.2.U55 2010
    368.4'2--dc22
                                                    2009042511

Printed in the United States of America
1 2 3 4 5 6 7 14 13 12 11 10

Contents

Chapter 2: Is Access to Health Care a Moral Issue?

Chapter 3: Does Universal Health Care Work in Other Countries?

Chapter 4: What Steps Can the U.S. Take to Achieve Universal Health Care?

Why Consider Opposing Viewpoints?

> *"The only way in which a human being can make some approach to knowing the whole of a subject is by hearing what can be said about it by persons of every variety of opinion and studying all modes in which it can be looked at by every character of mind. No wise man ever acquired his wisdom in any mode but this."*
>
> *John Stuart Mill*

In our media-intensive culture it is not difficult to find differing opinions. Thousands of newspapers and magazines and dozens of radio and television talk shows resound with differing points of view. The difficulty lies in deciding which opinion to agree with and which "experts" seem the most credible. The more inundated we become with differing opinions and claims, the more essential it is to hone critical reading and thinking skills to evaluate these ideas. *Opposing Viewpoints* books address this problem directly by presenting stimulating debates that can be used to enhance and teach these skills. The varied opinions contained in each book examine many different aspects of a single issue. While examining these conveniently edited opposing views, readers can develop critical thinking skills such as the ability to compare and contrast authors' credibility, facts, argumentation styles, use of persuasive techniques, and other stylistic tools. In short, the *Opposing Viewpoints* series is an ideal way to attain the higher-level thinking and reading skills so essential in a culture of diverse and contradictory opinions.

In addition to providing a tool for critical thinking, *Opposing Viewpoints* books challenge readers to question their own strongly held opinions and assumptions. Most people form their opinions on the basis of upbringing, peer pressure, and personal, cultural, or professional bias. By reading carefully balanced opposing views, readers must directly confront new ideas as well as the opinions of those with whom they disagree. This is not to simplistically argue that everyone who reads opposing views will—or should—change his or her opinion. Instead, the series enhances readers' understanding of their own views by encouraging confrontation with opposing ideas. Careful examination of others' views can lead to the readers' understanding of the logical inconsistencies in their own opinions, perspective on why they hold an opinion, and the consideration of the possibility that their opinion requires further evaluation.

Evaluating Other Opinions

To ensure that this type of examination occurs, *Opposing Viewpoints* books present all types of opinions. Prominent spokespeople on different sides of each issue as well as well-known professionals from many disciplines challenge the reader. An additional goal of the series is to provide a forum for other, less known, or even unpopular viewpoints. The opinion of an ordinary person who has had to make the decision to cut off life support from a terminally ill relative, for example, may be just as valuable and provide just as much insight as a medical ethicist's professional opinion. The editors have two additional purposes in including these less known views. One, the editors encourage readers to respect others' opinions—even when not enhanced by professional credibility. It is only by reading or listening to and objectively evaluating others' ideas that one can determine whether they are worthy of consideration. Two, the inclusion of such viewpoints encourages the important critical thinking skill of objectively evaluating an author's credentials and bias. This evaluation will illuminate an author's reasons for taking a particular stance on an issue and will aid in readers' evaluation of the author's ideas.

It is our hope that these books will give readers a deeper understanding of the issues debated and an appreciation of the complexity of even seemingly simple issues when good and honest people disagree. This awareness is particularly important in a democratic society such as ours in which people enter into public debate to determine the common good. Those with whom one disagrees should not be regarded as enemies but rather as people whose views deserve careful examination and may shed light on one's own.

Thomas Jefferson once said that "difference of opinion leads to inquiry, and inquiry to truth." Jefferson, a broadly educated man, argued that "if a nation expects to be ignorant and free . . . it expects what never was and never will be." As individuals and as a nation, it is imperative that we consider the opinions of others and examine them with skill and discernment. The *Opposing Viewpoints* series is intended to help readers achieve this goal.

David L. Bender and Bruno Leone,
Founders

Introduction

"Health care is a service that we all need, but just like food and shelter it is best provided through voluntary and mutually beneficial market exchanges."

John Mackey,
CEO of Whole Foods,
Wall Street Journal,
August 12, 2009

"Universal health care needs to happen not because it is a right, but because as a society we together believe that everyone should have access to at least a minimum level of medical assistance when they need it. It's a moral issue."

"Beargulch":
anonymous response to John Mackey's
WSJ opinion piece published
at wellness.blogs.time.com
on August 14, 2009

When John Mackey, the cofounder and CEO of Whole Foods Market, Inc., laid out his eight best ideas for health care reform in a *Wall Street Journal* opinion piece in August 2009, the response was swift. Within days, a four-thousand-member group had coalesced on Facebook, promoting a boycott of the store to protest Mackey's statement. Two weeks later, the "Boycott Whole Foods" group had grown to almost twenty-four-thousand members. Wellness blogs across the Internet were filled with angry retorts to Mackey's views from people who identified themselves as once-loyal Whole Foods shoppers and investors. "As a customer, I am glad that

Whole Foods now has competitors," one customer wrote on *Time* magazine's Wellness blog. "If Mr. Mackey wants to be a strict free-marketer, then he can deal with the consequences of me no longer buying his product. As a stockholder, I am livid that Mr. Mackey drags Whole Foods in the middle of a fight to advance his personal neo-conservative agenda."

John Mackey posted a statement on his blog emphasizing that the ideas he shared were his own personal opinions, and that Whole Foods Market does not have an official position on health care reform. "As we, as a nation, continue to discuss this," he said, "I am hopeful that both sides can do so in a civil manner that will lead to positive change for all concerned." He reposted the text of the *Wall Street Journal* article. Mackey believes his proposed policy reforms, which include removing the tax advantage for employer-sponsored health insurance, allowing insurance companies to sell policies across state lines, and incentivizing high-deductible policies and health savings accounts, would result in lower health care costs.

The debate Mackey stirred up on the Internet and in newspapers mirrored what was going on elsewhere in the summer of 2009, as the wish for civil discussion seemed, in many places, to go unfulfilled. When town hall meetings were scheduled to take the issue of health care reform to local communities, media coverage focused on protestors who arrived at events with loaded guns strapped to their thighs, or who carried posters featuring retouched photographs of President Barack Obama sporting a Hitler-style mustache.

When a woman at a town hall meeting asked Massachusetts Congressman Barney Frank why he was supporting a Nazi-inspired health care bill, Frank, who is Jewish, shot back, "On what planet do you spend most of your time?" and did not try to hide his irritation. Supporters of health care reform complained that protestors were drowning out legitimate debate. In some places town hall meetings were cancelled, out of fear that they would become violent.

John Mackey's effort to articulate a vision for health care reform, and the response of some of his customers, illuminate basic issues at the heart of the health care debate. Mackey has long been a high-profile champion of the idea that corporations have social responsibilities that go beyond profit alone, and Whole Foods Market has worked hard to define its identity in terms of the value it places on relationships. The mission statement of Whole Foods Market, Inc., declares "Our ability to instill a clear sense of interdependence among our various stakeholders [the people who are interested and benefit from the success of our company] is contingent upon our efforts to communicate more often, more openly and more compassionately." The company strives to give both its employees and its customers a real, if limited, voice in corporate governance.

Employees receive, as part of their compensation, high-deductible (approximately $2,500) health insurance policies and an $1,800 per year health savings account that can be carried over from year to year if it is not used. Mackey's *Wall Street Journal* opinion piece stressed his belief that structuring health coverage in this way gives employees more power and encourages them to be more responsible in their use of health care dollars.

Against this background, Mackey's statement that a close reading of America's founding documents "will not reveal any intrinsic right to health care, food, or shelter," appears to be the cause of much of the negative backlash to his ideas. *Washington Post* columnist Ezra Kline criticized that statement by suggesting that food and health care are, in fact, similar. "We worry if people don't have enough food to eat," he wrote in an August 2009 column, "so we have a variety of programs meant to ensure that people have sufficient food." About 11 percent of the U.S. population receives food stamps, and millions are enrolled in WIC, the federal government's Women, Infants, and Children nutrition program. Low-income children receive reduced-price school lunches. "The insight that people need food [has] led us to solve, or try and solve, the problem directly by giving people money to buy food," Kline wrote.

A *Huffington Post* blogger and self-proclaimed Whole Foods devotee characterized Mackey's position as "disappointing." "Until [he] learns that truly declaring interdependence means that we take care of each other no matter what, I am not going to support his cognitive dissonance on interdependence with any more of my hard-earned local-organic-neo-hippie-spinach money."

Is access to health care a human right, or a valued social good, or neither? In 2003 the Institute of Medicine published a report, *Insuring America's Health*, which contained five principles for evaluating various strategies for health care reform. The first principle, "the most basic and important," was that health care coverage should be universal. The idea that access to health care should be universal, however, has become one of the most hotly debated issues in the ongoing discussion of how to reform the U.S. health care system. In *Opposing Viewpoints: Universal Health Care*, authors explore the complexities of the debate in the following chapters: Is the U.S. Health Care System Failing? Is Access to Health Care a Moral Issue? Does Universal Health Care Work in Other Countries? What Steps Can the U.S. Take to Achieve Universal Health Care? The diverse viewpoints that follow offer insight into the reasons for such impassioned debate over health care for all.

OPPOSING
VIEWPOINTS®
SERIES

CHAPTER 1

Is the U.S. Health Care System Failing?

Chapter Preface

Soon after Barack Obama became president-elect of the United States, in December 2008, he proclaimed his intention to reform the country's health care system. The United States was facing a $1.3 trillion budget deficit and a crisis in the financial system that was unprecedented in U.S. history. "Some may ask how at this moment of economic challenge we can afford to invest in reforming our health care system," President-elect Obama said, "I ask . . . how can we afford not to."[1]

That the U.S. health care system is broken and needs to be fixed is widely agreed to be true. In January 2009, for example, Michael Leavitt, who was ending four years as secretary of health and human services for the George W. Bush administration, came to a similar conclusion, predicting that the average American household's health care spending, including the portion of taxes paid for Medicare and Medicaid, would go from 23 percent to 41 percent of average household income over the next two decades if steps were not taken to address the situation. Leavitt's views were outlined in an opinion piece that month by *Washington Post* columnist George Will. Part of the problem, as Leavitt explained it, is that health care costs are not transparent. Consumers cannot get prices up front for common procedures, which makes it difficult to comparison shop. As a result, the system is bloated and unresponsive to consumer demand.

Leavitt called rapidly increasing health care costs "a nation-ruining issue." He predicted that the economic downturn would make the situation worse by shrinking tax revenues, resulting in the exhaustion of the Medicare Part A trust fund by 2016, three years earlier than had been previously predicted.

1. Joanne Kenen and Sarah Axeen, "The Cost of Doing Nothing on Health Care," *The American Prospect*, December 12, 2008.

What really concerned him, though, was the threat that long-term care for the indigent elderly posed to U.S. prosperity. Leavitt believes that many low-income elderly people shed their assets to become eligible for Medicaid and that states, eager to receive federal funds, often adjust Medicaid's requirements to increase the number of people who meet Medicaid eligibility requirements.

The idea that there is a "cost of doing nothing," is one that is frequently heard on both sides of the health care debate. When President-elect Obama stressed that need to reform health care, he relied in part on a report by the New America Foundation, which estimated that cost to be about $200 billion a year, and rising.

Conservatives like Michael Leavitt often stress that the coming increases in health care costs are unaffordable. For them, health care reform is entitlement reform, reducing the number of individuals who depend on the government for care. Those who agree with Obama, on the other hand, often argue that one of the benefits of covering more people will be economies of scale that will result in health care becoming more affordable for most people.

Is the U.S. health care system broken? Or is it stronger and less in need of reform than some have suggested? What kind of changes are under consideration? What are the real costs of various reforms, and how do they compare with the "cost of doing nothing?" These are some of the questions that will be considered in this chapter.

> *"Health care costs burden American employers, who are forced to cut back on providing coverage and benefits or suffer a competitive disadvantage against international companies who don't bear health costs."*

The U.S. Health Care System Needs to Change

Ben Furnas

Ben Furnas is a research associate at the Center for American Progress Action Fund, a progressive think tank. In this viewpoint, he argues that the U.S. health care system must be reformed. Per-person costs for health care in the United States have risen steadily in recent years to become a burden for families and a source of weakness for the economy as a whole. Yet in spite of excessive costs, the quality of health care in the United States has been declining, so that it now ranks behind almost every other industrialized country. Health care reform could lead to billions of dollars in savings.

Ben Furnas, "American Health Care Since 1994: The Unacceptable Status Quo," *Center for American Progress*, January 2009. Copyright © 2009 Center for American Progress. This material was created by the Center for American Progress www.americanprogress.org.

As you read, consider the following questions:

1. According to the author, how much has the per-person cost of health care in the United States increased since 1994?

2. How does the per capita cost of health care in the United States compare with that of Norway?

3. How many uninsured people lived in the United States in 2007, according to the Commonwealth Fund?

2009 presents a rare opportunity for health care reformers to achieve their goals of affordable, accessible, and effective health care for all. American families and businesses are ready for sweeping changes after years of skyrocketing costs, increasing numbers of uninsured, and inconsistent quality of care. President-elect Barack Obama has promised to make health care a top priority, and congressional majorities are eager to pass reform.

Fifteen years ago, the United States had a similar opportunity to reform health care. But conservatives and insurance industry lobbyists defeated Bill Clinton's efforts by claiming the plan would "socialize medicine," and arguing that there was "no health care crisis." Today, their successors are making the very same arguments against Barack Obama's plan.

If opponents of reform succeed, the next 15 years are likely to resemble the last 15. The result is predictable: higher and higher costs for a health care system that leaves out more and more people. Like today, businesses will be burdened with spiraling costs, states will spend more for safety nets for high-risk populations and the uninsured, and the whole system will encourage excessive and unnecessary spending while leaving millions behind.

Looking back at the last 15 years, we can assess the quality of the American health care system and how we got here. Examining the consequences of the 1994 failure to reform health care should be a stark warning for those who would once again choose to continue our deeply flawed health care system.

Rising Costs

Since 1994, the cost per person of American health care has more than doubled, with an annual growth rate regularly more than twice that of inflation. Fueled by rising costs of prescription drugs, inefficient outpatient care, expensive and unnecessary medical procedures, and ballooning insurance premiums, these costs are a burden on state and federal governments, businesses, and families.

Per-person health care expenditures in the United States have risen 6.5 percent per year since 2000, and 5.5 percent per year on average since 1994. In contrast, consumer inflation has averaged just 2.6 percent per year.

Health care costs burden American employers, who are forced to cut back on providing coverage and benefits or suffer a competitive disadvantage against international companies who don't bear health costs. Premiums for employer-provided health care have doubled since 2000 (the earliest year the Medical Expenditures Panel Survey has on record). That year the average family premium was $6,800. By 2008, it had risen to $12,700. This premium growth eats away at wages and pressures firms to reduce coverage.

The share of American firms offering health benefits shrank to 60 percent today [in 2009], from 66 percent in 1999. And the percentage of Americans covered through their employers, where coverage is of a much higher quality than in the individual market, was 59 percent in 2007, down from 64 percent in 1999. Without workplace health insurance, Americans must struggle to find coverage in the unregulated private market (where people with pre-existing conditions find it difficult or impossible to secure coverage), go on public assistance, or become uninsured.

Our productive capacity is suffering, too. The United States spent approximately 16 percent of its 2006 gross domestic product on health care, up from 8 percent in 1975. Without reform, the Congressional Budget Office [CBO] projects that health expenditures will rise to 25 percent of GDP by 2025. Health care spending among other rich, developed countries in the Organisation for Economic Cooperations and Development [OECD] averaged just 9 percent of GDP in 2006.

A Burden for Families

These costs are increasingly painful for American families, who face higher premiums, deductibles, and co-pays. According to Bureau of Labor Statistics consumer expenditure data, the share of household income spent on medical expenses has crept up since 1994. A recent study by the Commonwealth Fund found that, "accelerated growth in health care spending has translated into increased burdens on family budgets." According to the most recent data, an average of 13 million families (11 percent of American families) spent 10 percent or more on out-of-pocket health care expenses in 2000–01. That's up from 8 percent in 1996–97.

American spending on health care is wildly out of sync with other large developed economies. A recent McKinsey study found that the United States spent $650 billion more on health care than peer OECD countries even after adjusting for wealth.

Americans spend well over twice as much as the OECD median in annual per-person health care expenditures, and around 150 percent of the next highest-spending country. In 2006 (the most recent data available), the United States spent $6,700 per capita on health care, over double the OECD median expenditure of $3,100. Norway, the second biggest spender, spent $4,500 per person.

A Weight on the Economy

Higher medical costs are also taking a toll on America's fiscal health. As the CBO has warned, "the rate at which health care spending grows relative to the economy is the most important determinant of the country's long-term fiscal balance." Federal health care expenditures, including Medicare and Medicaid, have risen to over $800 billion, or $2,650 per person, in 2008, from $300 billion, or $1,600 per person, in 1994 (in constant 2008 dollars). The burden on states has increased as well, to $300 billion in health care costs in 2008, from $190 billion in 1994 (including each state's share of the Medicaid program). These trends are projected to speed up, with per-person federal expenditure nearing $6,000 by 2017 and state and local expenditures projected to increase to $2,000 per person (in 2008 dollars) over the same period.

While some of this increase is attributable to population growth, an aging population, and changes to the policy structures of Medicare and Medicaid (including an expansion of the State Children's Health Insurance Program), much of it comes from the underlying inefficiencies and excess costs of the American health care system.

Vanishing Coverage

Despite surging expenditures, the number of Americans going without insurance has risen to 46 million, or 15 percent of the population in 2007, up from 38 million, or 14 percent, in 1999. Among people aged 18–65, the uninsurance rate increased to almost 20 percent in 2007, up from 17 percent in 1999. If the 1999 rate had stayed constant, 4.5 million more American adults would have health insurance today.

In 36 states, the percentage of adults aged 18–65 going without health insurance has increased since 1999. Millions more are living with subpar or insufficient coverage. The Commonwealth Fund found that in 2007 there were "an estimated 25 million underinsured adults in the United States, up

Employer and Employee Health Insurance Costs Are Rising

- Premiums for employer-based health insurance rose by 5.0 percent in 2008. In 2007, small employers saw their premiums, on average, increase 5.5 percent. Firms with fewer than 24 workers experienced an increase of 6.8 percent.

- The annual premium that a health insurer charges an employer for a health plan covering a family of four averaged $12,700 in 2008. Workers contributed nearly $3,400, or 12 percent more than they did in 2007. The annual premiums for family coverage significantly eclipsed the gross earnings for a full-time, minimum-wage worker ($10,712). . . .

- Health insurance expenses are the fastest-growing cost component for employers.

"Health Insurance Costs,"
National Coalition on Health Care, 2009.
www.nchc.org.

60 percent from 2003." Underinsured adults "have health coverage that does not adequately protect them from high medical expenses," and they regularly go without needed care, leading to higher medical costs down the road.

The uninsured typically get care in the most expensive way: through hospitals and last-minute emergency care. These additional costs drive up premiums for those with health insurance. A 2005 Families USA study found that, by 2010, $1,500 of the cost of a family insurance premium will be due to costs associated with uncompensated care for the uninsured.

Declining Quality

It would be one thing if America's massive health care expenditures since 1994 were yielding first-rate results in health outcomes and the quality of care. Unfortunately, this isn't the case. In practically every international comparative measure of health quality, the United States lags behind other developed nations who spend just a fraction of what America does on health care.

A recent Commonwealth Fund study found that across 37 indicators covering quality, access, efficiency, and equity, the United States achieves "an overall score of 65 out of a possible 100 when comparing national averages with benchmarks of best performance achieved internationally and within the United States." In other words, the United States as a whole is performing well below the standards of health, efficiency, and care that are realistic and have been achieved in the most successful U.S. states and other developed nations. And the trends are pointing in the wrong direction: "On those indicators for which trend data exist, performance compared with benchmarks more often worsened than improved . . . between the 2006 and 2008 Scorecards."

One indicator of America's declining health care quality is infant mortality. In 1994, America's infant mortality rate (measured as infant deaths per 1,000 births) was 0.8 deaths below the OECD average of 8.8. By 2004, it was more than 1 death above the OECD average. Despite enormous per-person health expenditures, the United States ranks 26th in the world in infant mortality, behind the Slovak Republic and just ahead of Poland.

Life expectancy at birth shows the same pattern. In 2004 (the most recent data available), the United States ranked 23rd in the world in life expectancy, and it has been falling relative to the OECD average since 1994. In 2003, the United States fell to last place among 19 industrialized nations in mortality from cases that "might have been prevented with timely and effective care," according to a 2008 wide-reaching study from the Commonwealth Fund. The study found that "101,000 fewer people would die prematurely each year from causes amenable to health care if the U.S. achieved the lower mortality rates of leading countries."

Obesity rates, a key indicator of chronic conditions like heart disease and diabetes, have risen steadily since 1994, too. The percentage of Americans considered obese rose to 26.3 percent in 2007, from 16 percent in 1995. Effective chronic disease management and preventive care have been woefully neglected as a national priority and should be a key piece of any comprehensive and effective reforms.

Life expectancy varies wildly within the United States, from region to region, and across racial and class lines. A report by the Harvard School of Public Health found that "the gap between the highest and lowest life expectancies for race-county combinations in the United States is over 35 years." Working to reduce these disparities would go a long way toward raising overall performance and improving cost-effectiveness and health outcomes.

Billions Could Be Saved

Furthermore, within the United States, standards of care vary widely. Correcting these internal inequities would save the United States billions of dollars and improve the health of millions of Americans. To give just one example, in the typical U.S. state, 40 percent of people [older than] 50 receive the recommended screenings and preventive care. In the top five states, that rate is 50 percent, and in the lowest performing states, that rate is 30 percent. Making the worst states perform as well as the best states in this and the other benchmarks Commonwealth identifies (by improving access to primary care and expanding investment in prevention) would help 70 million more adults get the preventive care they need, which will both save money and improve health.

The status quo of American health care is spending more money to cover fewer people, yielding disappointing outcomes. Effective reforms, which would invest in measures to improve the quality and delivery of care, reform payment to reward outcomes, and provide affordable, accessible, comprehensive health insurance for all Americans, are long overdue. The best time to fix American health care was [more than] a decade ago. The second best time is now.

> "Estimates for the cost of a new national health care program run from $65 billion to $600 billion per year . . . money that would ultimately come out of the pockets of hard-working men and women."

Americans Have Much to Lose If the U.S. Health Care System Is Changed

Michael D. Tanner

Michael Tanner, a senior fellow at the Cato Institute, heads research into a variety of domestic policy issues. He is the author of Leviathan on the Right: How Big-Government Conservativism Brought Down the Republican Revolution *(2007). In this viewpoint, Tanner argues that although the U.S. health care system has problems, there are also serious dangers in reforming the present system. Americans could lose the power to choose their doctors and to choose among alternative treatments, and they could pay much higher taxes if the health care system is reformed as some have suggested.*

As you read, consider the following questions:

1. According to the author, how would a proposed Federal Health Board limit the power of individuals to choose their own treatments?

2. What reasons does the author give for the fact that some physicians are refusing to take new Medicare and Medicaid patients?

3. The United States has been the leader in medical innovation for many years. What are some of the examples of innovation cited in this viewpoint? How would a national health care system affect the United States' leading role in medical and pharmaceutical innovation, according to the author?

Americans are frustrated with our current health care system and clamoring for reform. This is no surprise in view of high costs, uneven quality, and the millions of Americans without health insurance. But not all change is change for the better. And before we head down the road to a government-run health care system, we need to stop and think about what we stand to lose.

Things to Think About

- You could lose your current insurance. Are you happy with your insurance? Too bad. Most of the proposals currently being considered, including one by Senate Finance Committee Chairman Max Baucus (D-MT), would mandate that all Americans purchase an insurance plan that contained a government-designed minimum benefits package. You may be perfectly satisfied with the insurance you have today, but if the government bureaucrats didn't think it was good enough, you would have to give up your current policy, and buy the one they wanted—even if it was more expensive or contained benefits you would never use.

Government-Run Health Care Is Not the Answer

Government-run health care—what proponents now euphemistically call "single-payer"—is not poised to sweep the body politic this year and transform the nation. Indeed, it is an idea that exists in the shadows. When Oregon voted in 2002 on a ballot initiative promising Canadian-style health care, voters in the liberal bastion responded with uncharacteristic resolve. Measure 23 was defeated by a 4 to 1 margin.

A few months later, Congressman John Conyers proposed the United States National Health Insurance Act. The response was equally unenthused in the nation's capital. Even the sympathetic *New York Times* failed to run a single story on the motion.

David Gratzer,
"Why Isn't Government Health Care the Answer?"
Freemarket Cure, 2007. www.freemarketcure.com.

- You could lose the power for you and your doctor to decide what treatment you will receive. Tom Daschle, the incoming Secretary of Health and Human Services [HHS], who is expected to lead President [Barack] Obama's drive for national health care, has called for the creation of a Federal Health Board with the power to determine what treatments and procedures are "cost-effective." [After this article was published, Tom Daschle withdrew his name from consideration for the HHS position because of tax irregularities.]

These standards would be imposed on programs directly funded by the federal government initially, but could be extended to private insurance in the future.

He acknowledges that "[d]octors and patients might resent any encroachment on their ability to choose certain treatments even if they are expensive or ineffectual compared to alternatives." No matter—government knows best.

- You could lose the ability to spend your own money for the health care you want. Many government-run health care programs limit the ability of individuals to purchase medical services with their own money. The practice exists today, in the federal Medicare program where the government effectively prohibits Medicare beneficiaries from going outside the program to obtain higher quality care or maintain medical privacy.

  And many advocates of national health care are opposed to a "two-tier" system under which some individuals could opt out of the government program to purchase their own care.

- You could lose your current doctor. A combination of excessive bureaucracy and low reimbursement under current government-run health care programs like Medicare and Medicaid is causing an increasing number of physicians to refuse to participate in those programs. According to the American Academy of Family Physicians, 17 percent of family doctors refuse to take new Medicare patients. A 2006 report from the Center for Studying Health System Change found that nearly half of all doctors polled said they had stopped accepting or limited the number of new Medicaid patients.

- You could lose access to the latest drugs and medical advancements. The U.S. has long led the world in medical and pharmaceutical research. Of all the new drugs introduced world wide over the past 30 years, more than half were patented in the U.S. And 80 percent of non-pharmaceutical medical innovations, like MRIs and transplants, were first introduced in this country. But national health care would impose price controls and practice guidelines that would significantly reduce research and development.

A study by the Manhattan Institute suggests that imposing price controls on prescription drugs, for example, would reduce research and development spending by $373 billion, eventually resulting in the loss of 277 million life years.

- And, of course, higher taxes. Estimates for the cost of a new national health care program run from $65 billion to $600 billion per year. While this may not sound like much in an era of $700 billion bailouts, it is still money that would ultimately come out of the pockets of hard-working men and women. Nor should we forget that such projections almost always underestimate the cost of those programs. When Medicare started back in 1965, the government thought it might cost as much as $9 billion by 1990. The actual cost that year: $65 billion.

Advocates of national health care frequently try to sell it as the proverbial "free lunch." And, given the problems facing our current health care system, many Americans may feel that nothing could be worse than what we have now. Why not take a chance—what is there to lose?

Quite a lot.

> *"A famine never strikes everyone equally. In a famine, the have-nots become the have-nothings while the haves become the have-barely-enoughs. And, as always, the wealthy survive."*

Too Many People Do Not Have Health Insurance

Clark Newhall

Clark Newhall, a physician and a medical malpractice attorney, argues in this viewpoint that America is suffering from a catastrophic failure of its health care system. America's privately run, for-profit health care industry has created massive inefficiencies and inequalities. One-third of every health care dollar goes to pay for marketing and administrative costs connected with running the health care and insurance businesses, and for CEO bonuses, while millions of people go without any health care at all. It is a crisis of biblical proportions. The best solution to the health care famine is a Medicare-like system that would provide health care for everyone.

Clark Newhall, "America's Health Care Famine Is Slowly Killing Us," *Salt Lake Tribune,* January 3, 2009. Reproduced by permission of the author. Attribute to Clark Newhall MD JD, Founder, Health-Justice.org.

As you read, consider the following questions:

1. Why does the author say that America is suffering from a health care famine? What are some of the elements of the current crisis that make it like a famine?

2. What are some of the unnecessary costs that are built into the current for-profit health care system, according to the author?

3. According to the author, how many people die each year because they cannot afford health insurance?

We don't have a health-care problem. We don't have a health-care crisis. What we have is a health-care famine.

I realized this when a friend told me that she was not in favor of universal health insurance. She was opposed to paying for health care for all. She has a little boy with cancer. She was afraid that universal health care would mean her little boy would not be able to get an appointment with the oncologist.

"But all those other children with cancer deserve treatment, too, don't they?" I asked. "I guess so," she grudgingly admitted, "but I have to worry about my little boy."

Too many other people's children would be trying to get appointments and treatment. Too many other people would be competing for a scarce resource—the time of a doctor.

It is a health-care famine.

Perhaps you know the story of Jacob, who predicted seven years of plenty and seven years of famine.[1] When famine came, he was prepared with full granaries. His brothers, who had sold him into slavery, begged him for grain for their starving families and he gave them grain. We are like Jacob's brothers in the famine, begging for health care. But for us, there is no Jacob. There is only the for-profit medical-industrial complex, gate-keeping us out of the health-care system.

1. The author erroneously refers to the story of Jacob, rather than that of Jacob's son Joseph; the story is found in the book of Genesis, in the Bible.

Poverty and Health Care Are Intertwined

As financially strapped families struggle to cover basic needs such as food, shelter and the increasing cost of energy, health insurance often takes a back seat on the list of priorities. A National Health Survey conducted by the U.S. Centers for Disease Control and Prevention found more than 40 million people of all ages went without insurance at some point in 2005.

Sabriya Rice,
"Poverty and Poor Health Are Intertwined, Experts Say,"
CNN, September 24, 2006. www.cnn.com.

We Have a Health Care Famine

When too many people are fighting to get the scarce stuff to stay alive, whether the scarce stuff is food or health care, that is a famine.

When those of us who have barely enough are willing to sacrifice those others of us who have too little or none at all, that is a famine.

When our own situation is so desperate that we turn a blind eye to the more desperate situation of others, that is a famine.

When dog-eat-dog surpasses "do unto others" as the Golden Rule, that is a famine.

A famine never strikes everyone equally. In a famine, the have-nots become the have-nothings while the haves become the have-barely-enoughs. And, as always, the wealthy survive, even thrive, even profit, from the shortages that are killing others.

This famine is not new—it has been slowly building for years.

The price of our privately run, profit-driven medical-industrial complex has caused this famine. About one-third of every dollar going to health care pays for administrative costs—for utilization reviewers, for computer programmers, for advertising, for sales managers, for executives of all kinds, for billing clerks, for coding clerks, for CEO bonuses in the millions and hundreds of million—and for profits.

We are not talking about government waste. We are not talking about the cost of actually treating the sick and nurturing the healthy. We are talking only about the cost of running our profit-making health insurance industry.

One third of the health-care dollar—that amount is far more than enough to give excellent medical care to everyone in the nation. It is far more than enough to fund the (privately-owned) surgical centers and imaging centers and Lasik centers that sprout up on every corner. It is even more than the amount we have given to Wall Street to bail out financiers and bankers from their hubristic near-demise.

Millions Are Suffering

The famine has grown while insurance companies charge higher premiums and reduce coverage, while employers cut their contributions and increase deductibles, while legislators reduce Medicaid and Children's Health Insurance Program budgets, and on and on.

We are in a health-care famine. Millions of us are suffering and millions more will suffer soon. More than 20,000 people die each year in this famine because they cannot afford the price of for-profit health insurance.

The famine will not end until, like Jacob [Joseph], we open the granaries and give aid to the starving. The health-care famine will not end until we end the money-hoarding that health insurance companies call "reserves" and "administrative costs" and "profits."

It will not end until we open our blind eye and see the plight of our neighbor. It will not end until we learn that tolerating a profit-making middleman in the health-care system builds a wall between patient and doctor. It will not end until we learn that good things for everyone can only be accomplished by the will of everyone.

It will not end until we pay for health care in the same way that we pay for everything else that we value highly—our security, our freedom, our laws. It will not end until we have a national health-care system that covers everyone equally and is paid for by everyone equitably.

It is time for national single-payer health insurance. It is time to remove the profit-making middleman from medical care. It is time to see health care for the public good that it is and not for the profitable business it has become. Support Medicare for all.

> "Despite the media's tendency to depict the 45.7 million uninsured as a single, homogeneous group, the demographic character of these individuals cuts across age, ethnic, and socioeconomic categories."

The Media Have Exaggerated the Number of Americans Without Health Insurance

Sally Pipes

Sally Pipes is president and chief executive officer of the Pacific Research Institute, a San Francisco–based think tank. In this viewpoint she argues that the media have distorted the findings of a recent U.S. Census Bureau report by exaggerating the number of people who are without health insurance. Furthermore, the media often assume that many people who want health insurance are unable to get it when, in fact, there are large numbers of individuals who choose not to be insured, and for whom the cost of health insurance is not a factor.

As you read, consider the following questions:

1. According to the author, has the number of uninsured people increased or decreased in recent years?

2. How do workers in transition distort the Census Bureau's count of uninsured individuals?

3. What are some of the reasons a person might choose to be uninsured, according to the author?

Officials at the U.S. Census Bureau recently released new health insurance figures purporting to show that the number of Americans officially classified as uninsured in 2007 was 45.7 million, down from 47 million in 2006.

Despite the decline, the new figure is being spun as proof positive that America's healthcare system is still in awful shape. Advocates of socialized medicine are repeating it ad nauseam, arguing that the main problem with the country's health system is the massive uninsured population. After all, if a whopping 15 percent of the population is uninsured, then the current system must be failing.

As Dr. Oliver Fein of Physicians for a National Health Program wrote when the figure came out, "[t]he plight of the uninsured ... shows how the for-profit, private health insurance model of financing health care has outlived its usefulness."

The Numbers Are Misleading

But it's grossly misleading to use the Census Bureau number as an indication of a crisis. A closer look at the agency's survey methods reveals that the situation isn't nearly as bad as the pundits and the politicians would have you believe.

To generate this figure, the Census Bureau relied entirely on a questionnaire known as the Current Population Survey (CPS). The survey is intended to garner information about, among other things, the income, age, race, living situation, and, of course, health insurance status of individuals living in the United States.

As with any survey of this size and scope, the accuracy of the data it produces has substantial margins of error. As the Census Bureau itself explains in its annual report, "health insurance coverage is likely to be underreported on the Current Population Survey."

The Census Bureau doesn't tell us that 45.7 million people are chronically uninsured for the entire year. The agency has stated elsewhere that "the CPS estimate of the number of people without health insurance more closely approximates the number of people who are uninsured at a specific point in time during the year than the number of people uninsured for the entire year."

In other words, many of the survey respondents counted as "uninsured" may have experienced only a temporary interruption in their insurance. This circumstance is quite common. When workers quit or lose their job, they are technically uninsured. But they are usually in transition between one employer-provided insurance policy and another.

Despite the media's tendency to depict the 45.7 million uninsured as a single, homogeneous group, the demographic character of these individuals cuts across age, ethnic, and socioeconomic categories. Many are uninsured for reasons unrelated to cost and don't need to be "rescued" by mandatory socialized medicine.

Not All Uninsured Are the Same

We may be accustomed to thinking of the uninsured as low-income individuals and struggling families. But the Census Bureau data show that many are relatively affluent. Over 17.5 million—38 percent—of the uninsured make more than $50,000 a year. And 9.1 million have an annual income of over $75,000 a year.

How can this be? In part, it's because a number of financially comfortable young Americans choose not to purchase

Census Bureau Figures Are Misleading

The Census Bureau's 2007 report on the uninsured found that . . . 9.7 million . . . are non-citizens, 7.9 million . . . are under 24 years old, and over 9 million could afford insurance because they make at least $75,000 a year. That leaves roughly 19 million uninsured, a much smaller problem than the media . . . admit.

Julie A. Seymour,
"CBS Keeps Misleading Viewers on Millions of Uninsured,
Promotes Obama's 'Actions' on Health Care,"
Newsbusters, February 26, 2008. www.newsbusters.org.

health insurance. Known in the healthcare trade as the "invincibles"—because they're so sure they won't get sick—these young singles would rather keep their money than shell out for expensive monthly insurance premiums because of the many mandates and regulations place on insurers by the states.

This intentional avoidance of health insurance is quite common. According to the Commonwealth Fund, Americans age[s] 19–29 [constitute] one of the largest and fastest-growing segments of the uninsured population.

If the fact that over a third of the uninsured are pulling down more than $50,000 a year isn't shocking enough, how about this: Nearly 10 million uninsured aren't even U.S. citizens!

It's certainly unfortunate that these individuals don't have health insurance, of course. But they can still get free treatment in emergency rooms. And even a fully nationalized healthcare system would be unlikely to provide them with health insurance.

Another 14 million of the uninsured are fully eligible for government assistance through programs like Medicare, Medicaid, and S-CHIP.

How does that break down? A 2008 study by the Georgetown University Health Policy Institute showed that a whopping 70 percent of uninsured children are eligible for Medicaid, S-CHIP, or both programs. And roughly 27 percent of non-elderly Americans who are eligible for Medicaid haven't enrolled and simply live their lives without health insurance, according to the Urban Institute.

Some Choose Not to Be Covered

Is it really fair to say that such individuals don't have health insurance? Further, if millions of Americans aren't availing themselves of taxpayer-funded coverage, why should we think that an even bigger government healthcare bureaucracy would solve the problem?

Of course, there are people who really do fall through the cracks. These are the chronically uninsured—the working poor. They are people who struggle to hold down jobs and support their families. They earn less than $50,000 per year but too much to qualify for government help. They simply can't afford insurance.

There are roughly 8 million of these chronically uninsured. Any attempt to solve the problem of the uninsured should focus on this narrow slice of the 45.7-million-person pie.

The key to helping these people isn't to create more government red tape. In fact, too much regulation is why health insurance is so expensive in the first place. What these people need is straightforward, affordable coverage that will cover them in the event of a health catastrophe. They should be able to purchase insurance in the state that has the best plan for them, regardless of where they live.

It's true that far too many Americans go without health insurance. And that is a serious problem. But the Census Bureau figure shouldn't be presented as anything other than what it really is: an imprecise snapshot of a heterogeneous group of Americans, many of whom wouldn't benefit from additional government intrusion into the healthcare market.

> "If we want to get to real reform, we have to change the open-ended payment policies of private insurance, Medicare, and Medicaid, the three principal financing sources that now funnel money to physicians, hospitals, and other providers."

Open-Ended Insurance Payments Encourage Abuse of the Health Care System

Robert B. Helms

Robert B. Helms is a resident scholar at the American Enterprise Institute, a think tank that seeks to advance the principles of limited government, private enterprise, and individual liberty. In this viewpoint he argues that the open-ended payments that are a common feature of private health insurance, Medicare, and Medicaid, are a primary source of out-of-control costs in health care. Open-ended payments encourage wasteful spending rather

Robert B. Helms, "Three Roadblocks to Health Reform," *American Enterprise Institute,* January 2009. Copyright © 2009 American Enterprise Institute for Public Policy Research. Reproduced with the permission of the American Enterprise Institute for Public Policy Research, Washington, D.C.

than rewarding a careful consideration of quality, value, cost, and benefit. Various proposals advocating a fixed payment system would offer higher quality and greater economic value in health care.

As you read, consider the following questions:

1. What are some of the factors that contributed to the demand for private health insurance after WWII?

2. In what way did Medicare imitate the private insurance industry when it was created?

3. How much do the states of Vermont, Rhode Island, New York, Nevada, Texas and Mississippi receive for each person on their Medicaid rolls? How does the author explain the differences among states?

The election is over and the health care reform debate has entered a new phase. President-elect [Barack] Obama has restated his commitment to health policy reform and has made several appointments to his new team of health policy leaders. Several members of Congress are issuing new health reform plans and jockeying to be leaders in what many are saying is the best chance for health reform in decades.

If history is any guide, the road to health care reform will not be an easy one. Presidents [Harry] Truman, [Jimmy] Carter, [Ronald] Reagan, [Bill] Clinton, and Bush [G. W.] have all proposed comprehensive reforms that have all been rejected by Congress. President [Lyndon B.] Johnson succeeded in getting Medicare and Medicaid passed in 1965, but these were new public programs for the aged, poor, and the disabled, not an overall reform of the health care system.

In fact, many health policy analysts point out that Medicare and Medicaid adopted the basic payment policies of private insurance, thereby making overall reform even more difficult. As we have seen time and again, making a lot of noise about health reform does not guarantee change.

What do we want from reform, and what will it take to get us there? To answer this question and see why reform is so difficult, let us look at the three largest components of our health care system—private health insurance, Medicare, and Medicaid—and look at how they work. Each of these major sectors of our health care system creates a roadblock to reform. Each is an open-ended system of payment that encourages everyone involved—consumers and providers—to use more resources than they would in a more normal, less-insured market.

First Roadblock: Private Health Insurance

In 2007, private health insurance and direct payments by individuals accounted for 46 percent ($1.04 trillion) of total health expenditures ($2.3 trillion). The modern form of private health insurance began in the 1930s, but the industry's major growth occurred after World War II. The percentage of those with hospital coverage increased from 10 percent (12.3 million) in 1940 to almost 90 percent (178 million) by 1975.

Modern drugs and new medical knowledge increased the demand for medical care. But since medical care was expensive to only a small number of sick people, it created an opportunity for the development of commercial health insurance. Consumers could agree [to] the payment of a relatively small premium in exchange for the promise of an insurance company to pay the larger costs of a medical event if such treatment became necessary. Increases in the population and higher family incomes also boosted demand for health insurance.

Furthermore, a somewhat unintended change in tax policy made it advantageous to acquire health insurance through employers rather than as individuals, as one might do with life, fire, or auto insurance. During WWII the National War Labor Board excluded the value of employer-provided health insurance from its wartime wage controls.

An unintended consequence of this policy was to induce employers to offer more health insurance as a way around the limits on wages. After the war, this tax treatment effectively lowered taxes for those American workers who could get health insurance from their employer. As a result, the exclusion of the value of employer-provided health insurance from taxable income increased the demand for employer-based health insurance relative to individual insurance. Since the tax exclusion was open-ended, it created strong incentives for employees and unions to bargain for more extensive coverage (more coverage of physician care, drugs, mental health, etc.) and less cost-sharing.

This kind of health insurance covered more people and more medical services, but did so in a way that encouraged more expenditure with little regard to the cost-effectiveness or value of the services. The tax treatment of health insurance is still open-ended, giving employers and insurers little reason to develop more cost-effective health insurance policies.

Second Roadblock: Medicare

The second major sector of our health care system is Medicare, the government program providing health care for the aged and the disabled. In 2007, Medicare expenditures accounted for 20 percent ($444.7 billion) of total health expenditures. Medicare originally adopted the payment policies used by private insurance in the 1960s, the practice of paying the cost of the claims submitted by licensed physicians and hospitals. This fee-for-service system is still in place for about 82 percent of the Medicare population. The remaining 18 percent are in the Medicare version of managed care.

Like private health insurance, Medicare's fee-for-service payment system is open-ended. As such, it creates incentives to submit more claims as a way of receiving more payment. The more the government clamps down on payment rates, the greater the incentive to submit more claims. Thus, spending

Improving Health Care Value: Quality and Cost

BCBSA [BlueCross and BlueShield Association] strongly recommends that Congress pass legislation creating a new institute that would support research comparing the effectiveness of new and existing procedures, drugs, devices, and biologics [pharmaceutical components found in nature] based on four key principles:

1. funding should be ensured by asking all payers—government and private—to contribute;

2. the institute should support a broad range of research, especially clinical trials;

3. significant education programs and incentives are needed; and

4. the new institute should be governed by a board with both public and private representation.

BlueCross BlueShield Association,
"Improving Health Care Value: Quality and Cost,"
September 25, 2007. www.bcbs.com.

rises with little worry about either the medical or economic effectiveness of the services. The result is very high increases in the cost of the program and dire predictions of impending bankruptcy.

Third Roadblock: Medicaid

The third major sector of our health care system is Medicaid, the joint federal and state program covering the poor and the disabled, including many of those in nursing homes. In 2007, Medicaid expenditures were 15 percent ($336.5 billion) of total health expenditures. Operating under federal rules, the states still have a lot of flexibility about how they run their state programs: who[m] they will cover, what benefits they will provide, and what payments they will make to providers. Compared to private insurance and Medicare, Medicaid programs in most states have the reputation of paying the lowest rates.

These frugal payment policies save some money but force many patients to seek care in hospital emergency rooms because they cannot find a physician that will accept Medicaid patients. The payment rules also bring about early and inappropriate admission of the aged and disabled to nursing homes when the rules do not allow them to use more cost-effective care to stay in their homes. The federal government and many of the states are trying to reduce inappropriate nursing home use through new programs.

Medicaid programs suffer from the same open-ended payment policies we have seen in the other two sectors—policies that encourage excessive use of services with little regard for their value. But this is not the only problem with Medicaid.

The program suffers from an additional open-ended payment policy that inflates the cost of the program at both the state and federal level. Medicaid is an open-ended entitlement funded by both the federal and the state governments. The federal government matches qualified state expenditures based on a formula that gives higher matching rates to states with lower levels of per capita income. In 2008, Mississippi got the highest matching rate, 76 percent, while 13 of the wealthiest states—such as New York and Connecticut—received the minimum matching rate of 50 percent. This payment policy, designed to advantage the low income states, ends up inducing the wealthier states to expand their program relative to the poorer states. This causes more federal dollars to flow to states with higher per capita incomes, not the states that have the largest populations of poor people and people without health insurance. For example, in 2006 Vermont received $7,753 in Federal Medicaid payments per poor person in poverty (state population at 125 percent or less of the federal poverty line), Rhode Island received $6,817, and New York received $6,462. At the other end of the scale, federal Medicaid dollars per poor person were $2,014 in Nevada, $2,150 in Texas, and $3,354 in Mississippi. This poor distribution of federal Medicaid dollars will continue to increase as long as the present open-ended payment policy continues.

Getting Around the Roadblocks to Real Health Care Reform

Medical and health policy journals are now full of articles, mostly written by physicians, about what is wrong with our present system and what it will take to reform it. These articles put major emphasis on the need to base medical decisions on new knowledge about medical outcomes and cost-effectiveness, on more attention to lifestyles and prevention, and the use of computers (IT) to improve efficiency.

These are obviously good ideas that would lead to improvement, but people must have an incentive to do these things before any real progress will be made. The present system of open-ended payment policies does not encourage this kind of change because it continues to reward wasteful spending rather than a careful consideration of costs and benefits. If we want to get to real reform, we have to change the open-ended payment policies of private insurance, Medicare, and Medicaid, the three principal financing sources that now funnel money to physicians, hospitals, and other providers.

There are many proposals designed to replace the existing open-ended payment policies with a fixed or limited payment. For example, to reform employer-based health insurance, the simplest proposal is to cap the amount of health insurance that a firm can provide tax free. This would create strong incentives for firms and insurance companies to redesign their health insurance policies so that their costs stay below the cap. Designing these more cost-effective policies would give everyone more reason to seriously consider the value of IT, prevention, and evidence on medical outcomes. More complicated proposals along these lines involve adding a refundable tax credit to assist low-income people to purchase health insurance.

Medicare reform proposals envision giving each eligible person a fixed voucher that could be used to purchase one of several federally approved health plans. Each plan would be required to cover a set of defined benefits and compete with other plans to provide quality service to Medicare beneficiaries.

Proposals to reform the Medicaid program also take a variety of approaches, all designed to provide a fixed payment to the individual or to the state. The federal formula could be modified to allocate federal money to the states based on each state's population of the poor and disabled. The states could also be given more incentives to use managed care plans that would have stronger incentives to effectively manage the care of the disabled and those with chronic conditions. State experiments have shown much promise for programs that allow more of these beneficiaries to receive care [at home] rather than in nursing homes.

What we all seem to want from health reform is a better system that will provide us with higher quality care and greater economic value. To achieve this kind of reform will require us to end the open-ended payment systems we now have and replace them with systems that reward quality and value. The longer we wait to start, the more difficult this kind of change will be.

> "A particular idea has taken hold among prominent American economists which has also been a powerful impediment to the expansion of health insurance. The idea is known as 'moral hazard.'"

Open-Ended Insurance Payments Do Not Lead to Abuse of the Health Care System

Malcolm Gladwell

Malcolm Gladwell has been a staff writer with The New Yorker *magazine since 1996. He is the author of several books, including "The Tipping Point: How Little Things Make a Big Difference" (2000) and "Blink: The Power of Thinking Without Thinking" (2005), both of which were bestsellers. In this viewpoint he argues that the concept of moral hazard—that the availability of health insurance will cause people to abuse the system—is the cause of much of the dysfunction in the U.S. health care system.*

As you read, consider the following questions:

1. According to the author, what is the leading cause of personal bankruptcy in the United States?

2. What is "moral hazard," and how does it influence thinking about health care spending?

3. What is the "social insurance" model of health care?

Several years ago, two Harvard researchers, Susan Starr Sered and Rushika Fernandopulle, set out to interview people without health-care coverage for a book they were writing, "Uninsured in America." They talked to as many kinds of people as they could find, collecting stories of untreated depression and struggling single mothers and chronically injured laborers—and the most common complaint they heard was about teeth. Gina, a hairdresser in Idaho, whose husband worked as a freight manager at a chain store, had "a peculiar mannerism of keeping her mouth closed even when speaking." It turned out that she hadn't been able to afford dental care for three years, and one of her front teeth was rotting. Daniel, a construction worker, pulled out his bad teeth with pliers. Then, there was Loretta, who worked nights at a university research center in Mississippi, and was missing most of her teeth. "They'll break off after a while, and then you just grab a hold of them, and they work their way out," she explained to Sered and Fernandopulle. "It hurts so bad, because the tooth aches. Then it's a relief just to get it out of there. The hole closes up itself anyway. So it's so much better."

People without health insurance have bad teeth because, if you're paying for everything out of your own pocket, going to the dentist for a checkup seems like a luxury. It isn't, of course . . . "Almost every time we asked interviewees what their first priority would be if the president established universal health coverage tomorrow," Sered and Fernandopulle write, "the immediate answer was 'my teeth.'"

Health Care in Crisis

The U.S. health-care system, according to "Uninsured in America," has created a group of people who increasingly look different from others and suffer in ways that others do not. The leading cause of personal bankruptcy in the United States is unpaid medical bills. Half of the uninsured owe money to hospitals, and a third are being pursued by collection agencies. Children without health insurance are less likely to receive medical attention for serious injuries, for recurrent ear infections, or for asthma. Lung-cancer patients without insurance are less likely to receive surgery, chemotherapy, or radiation treatment. Heart-attack victims without health insurance are less likely to receive angioplasty. People with pneumonia who don't have health insurance are less likely to receive X rays or consultations. The death rate in any given year for someone without health insurance is twenty-five per cent higher than for someone with insurance. . . .

One of the great mysteries of political life in the United States is why Americans are so devoted to their health-care system. Six times in the past century—during the First World War, during the Depression, during the [Harry S.] Truman and [Lyndon B.] Johnson Administrations, in the Senate in the nineteen-seventies, during the [Bill] Clinton years—efforts have been made to introduce some kind of universal health insurance, and each time the efforts have been rejected. Instead, the United States has opted for a makeshift system of increasing complexity and dysfunction. Americans spend $5,267 per capita on health care every year, almost two and half times the industrialized world's median of $2,193; the extra spending comes to hundreds of billions of dollars a year. What does that extra spending buy us? Americans have fewer doctors per capita than most Western countries. We go to the doctor less than people in other Western countries. We get admitted to the hospital less frequently than people in other Western countries. We are less satisfied with our health care than our counterparts in other countries. American life expectancy is lower than the Western average. Childhood-immunization rates in the United States are lower than average. Infant-mortality rates are in the nineteenth percentile of industrialized nations. Doctors here perform more high-end medical procedures, such as coronary angioplasties, than in other countries, but most of the wealthier Western countries have more CT scanners than the United States does, and Switzerland, Japan, Austria, and Finland all have more MRI machines per capita. Nor is our system more efficient. The United States spends more than a thousand dollars per capita per year—or close to four hundred billion dollars—on health-care-related paperwork and administration, whereas Canada, for example, spends only about three hundred dollars per capita. And, of course, every other country in the industrialized world insures all its citizens; despite those extra hundreds of billions of dollars we spend each year, we leave forty-five million people without any insurance. A country that displays an almost ruthless commitment to efficiency and performance in every aspect of its economy—a country that switched to Japanese cars the moment they were more reliable, and to Chinese T-shirts the moment they were five cents cheaper—has loyally stuck with a health-care system that leaves its citizenry pulling out their teeth with pliers.

A History of False Start

America's health-care mess is, in part, simply an accident of history. The fact that there have been six attempts at universal health coverage in the last century suggests that there has long been support for the idea. But politics has always got in the way. In both Europe and the United States, for example, the push for health insurance was led, in large part, by organized labor. But in Europe the unions worked through the political system, fighting for coverage for all citizens. From the start, health insurance in Europe was public and universal, and that created powerful political support for any attempt to expand benefits. In the United States, by contrast, the unions worked through the collective-bargaining system and, as a result, could win health benefits only for their own members. Health insurance here has always been private and selective, and every attempt to expand benefits has resulted in a paralyzing political battle over who would be added to insurance rolls and who ought to pay for those additions.

Policy is driven by more than politics, however. It is equally driven by ideas, and in the past few decades a particular idea has taken hold among prominent American economists which has also been a powerful impediment to the expansion of health insurance. The idea is known as "moral hazard." Health economists in other Western nations do not share this obsession. Nor do most Americans. But moral hazard has profoundly shaped the way think tanks formulate policy and the way experts argue and the way health insurers structure their plans and the way legislation and regulations have been written. The health-care mess isn't merely the unintentional result of political dysfunction, in other words. It is also the deliberate consequence of the way in which American policymakers have come to think about insurance.

"Moral hazard" is the term economists use to describe the fact that insurance can change the behavior of the person being insured. If your office gives you and your co-workers all the free Pepsi you want—if your employer, in effect, offers universal Pepsi insurance—you'll drink more Pepsi than you would have otherwise. If you have a no-deductible fire-insurance policy, you may be a little less diligent in clearing the brush away from your house. . . .

In 1968, the economist Mark Pauly argued that moral hazard played an enormous role in medicine, and, as John Nyman writes in his book *The Theory of the Demand for Health Insurance*, Pauly's paper has become the "single most influential article in the health economics literature." Nyman, an economist at the University of Minnesota, says that the fear of moral hazard lies behind the thicket of co-payments and deductibles and utilization reviews which characterizes the American health-insurance system. Fear of moral hazard, Nyman writes, also explains "the general lack of enthusiasm by U.S. health economists for the expansion of health insurance coverage (for example, national health insurance or expanded Medicare benefits) in the U.S."

What Nyman is saying is that when your insurance company requires that you make a twenty-dollar co-payment for a visit to the doctor, or when your plan includes an annual five-hundred-dollar or thousand-dollar deductible, it's not simply an attempt to get you to pick up a larger share of your health costs. It is an attempt to make your use of the health-care system more efficient. Making you responsible for a share of the costs, the argument runs, will reduce moral hazard: you'll no longer grab one of those free Pepsis when you aren't really thirsty. That's also why Nyman says that the notion of moral hazard is behind the "lack of enthusiasm" for expansion of health insurance. If you think of insurance as producing wasteful consumption of medical services, then the fact that there are forty-five million Americans without health insurance is no longer an immediate cause for alarm. After all, it's not as if the uninsured *never* go to the doctor. They spend, on average, $934 a year on medical care. A moral-hazard theorist would say that they go to the doctor when they really have to. Those of us with private insurance, by contrast, consume $2,347 worth of health care a year. If a lot of that extra $1,413 is waste, then maybe the uninsured person is the truly efficient consumer of health care.

The Moral Hazard Argument Doesn't Work with Health Care

The moral-hazard argument makes sense, however, only if we consume health care in the same way that we consume other

A Broken Connection

In recent years . . . the relationship between employment and health care has become increasingly problematic. First, as the nature of employment has changed globally, fewer people are able to stay in the same job for many years. As a result, jobs no longer serve as stable platforms for health care arrangements. Second, the fragmented nature of the American health care system, together with the political dominance of the medical, insurance, and pharmaceutical industries, has allowed health care costs to soar far above the costs for comparable products and services in Canada, Great Britain, and continental European countries. As the cost of health care rises, more employers look for ways to avoid providing insurance to their employees. The millions who find themselves uninsured are now priced out of the health care marketplace.

Susan Starr Sered and Rushika Fernandopulle,
"Introduction: The Death Spiral," Uninsured in America,
Beckley: University of California Press, 2005. www.ucpress.edu.

consumer goods, and to economists like Nyman this assumption is plainly absurd. We go to the doctor grudgingly, only because we're sick. "Moral hazard is overblown," the Princeton economist Uwe Reinhardt says. "You always hear that the demand for health care is unlimited. This is just not true. People who are very well insured, who are very rich, do you see them check into the hospital because it's free? Do people really like to go to the doctor? Do they check into the hospital instead of playing golf?"

For that matter, when you have to pay for your own health care, does your consumption really become more efficient? In the late nineteen-seventies, the Rand Corporation did an extensive study on the question, randomly assigning families to health plans with co-payment levels at zero per cent, twenty-five per cent, fifty per cent, or ninety-five per cent, up to six thousand dollars. As you might expect, the more that people were asked to chip in for their health care the less care they used. The problem was that they cut back equally on both frivolous care and useful care. Poor people in the high-deductible group with hypertension, for instance, didn't do nearly as good a job of controlling their blood pressure as those in other groups, resulting in a ten-per-cent increase in the likelihood of death. As a recent Commonwealth Fund study concluded, cost sharing is "a blunt instrument." Of course it is: how should the average consumer be expected to know beforehand what care is frivolous and what care is useful? I just went to the dermatologist to get moles checked for skin cancer. If I had had to pay a hundred per cent, or even fifty per cent, of the cost of the visit, I might not have gone. Would that have been a wise decision? I have no idea. But if one of those moles really is cancerous, that simple, inexpensive visit could save the health-care system tens of thousands of dollars (not to mention saving me a great deal of heartbreak). The focus on moral hazard suggests that the changes we make in our behavior when we have insurance are nearly always wasteful. Yet, when it comes to health care, many of the things we do only because we have insurance— like getting our moles checked, or getting our teeth cleaned regularly, or getting a mammogram or engaging in other routine preventive care—are anything but wasteful and inefficient. In fact, they are behaviors that could end up saving the health-care system a good deal of money. . . .

At the center of the [George W.] Bush Administration's plan to address the health-insurance mess are Health Savings Accounts, and Health Savings Accounts are exactly what you would come up with if you were concerned, above all else, with minimizing moral hazard. . . .

Health Savings Accounts Won't Solve the Problem

Under the Health Savings Accounts system, consumers are asked to pay for routine health care with their own money—several thousand dollars of which can be put into a tax-free account. To handle their catastrophic expenses, they then purchase a basic health-insurance package with, say, a thousand-dollar annual deductible. As President Bush explained recently, "Health Savings Accounts all aim at empowering people to make decisions for themselves, owning their own health-care plan, and at the same time bringing some demand control into the cost of health care."

The country described in the President's report is a very different place from the country described in "Uninsured in America." Sered and Fernandopulle look at the billions we spend on medical care and wonder why Americans have so little insurance. The President's report considers the same situation and worries that we have too much. Sered and Fernandopulle see the lack of insurance as a problem of poverty; a third of the uninsured, after all, have incomes below the federal poverty line. In the section on the uninsured in the President's report, the word "poverty" is never used. In the Administration's view, people are offered insurance but "decline the coverage" as "a matter of choice." The uninsured in Sered and Fernandopulle's book decline coverage, but only because they can't afford it. Gina, for instance, works for a beauty salon that offers her a bare-bones health-insurance plan with a thousand-dollar deductible for two hundred dollars a month. What's her total income? Nine hundred dollars a month. She could "choose" to accept health insurance, but only if she chose to stop buying food or paying the rent.

The biggest difference between the two accounts, though, has to do with how each views the function of insurance. Gina, Steve, and Loretta are ill, and need insurance to cover the costs of getting better. In their eyes, insurance is meant to help equalize financial risk between the healthy and the sick. In the insurance business, this model of coverage is known as "social insurance," and historically it was the way health coverage was conceived. If you were sixty and had heart disease and diabetes, you didn't pay substantially more for coverage than a perfectly healthy twenty-five-year-old. Under social insurance, the twenty-five-year-old agrees to pay thousands of dollars in premiums even though he didn't go to the doctor at all in the previous year, because he wants to make sure that someone else will subsidize his health care if he ever comes down with heart disease or diabetes. Canada and Germany and Japan and all the other industrialized nations with universal health care follow the social-insurance model. Medicare, too, is based on the social-insurance model, and, when Americans with Medicare report themselves to be happier with virtually every aspect of their insurance coverage than people with private insurance (as they do, repeatedly and overwhelmingly), they are referring to the social aspect of their insurance. They aren't getting better care. But they are getting something just as valuable: the security of being insulated against the financial shock of serious illness.

There is another way to organize insurance, however, and that is to make it actuarial. Car insurance, for instance, is actuarial. How much you pay is in large part a function of your individual situation and history: someone who drives a sports car and has received twenty speeding tickets in the past two years pays a much higher annual premium than a soccer mom with a minivan. In recent years, the private insurance industry in the United States has been moving toward the actuarial model, with profound consequences. The triumph of the actuarial model over the social-insurance model is the reason that companies unlucky enough to employ older, high-cost employees—like United Airlines—have run into such financial difficulty. It's the reason that automakers are increasingly moving their operations to Canada. It's the reason that small businesses that have one or two employees with serious illnesses suddenly face unmanageably high health-insurance premiums, and it's the reason that, in many states, people suffering from a potentially high-cost medical condition can't get anyone to insure them at all.

Health Savings Accounts represent the final, irrevocable step in the actuarial direction. If you are preoccupied with moral hazard, then you want people to pay for care with their own money, and, when you do that, the sick inevitably end up paying more than the healthy. . . . Health Savings Accounts are not a variant of universal health care. In their governing assumptions, they are the antithesis of universal health care.

The issue about what to do with the health-care system is sometimes presented as a technical argument about the merits of one kind of coverage over another or as an ideological argument about socialized versus private medicine. It is, instead, about a few very simple questions. Do you think that this kind of redistribution of risk is a good idea? Do you think that people whose genes predispose them to depression or cancer, or whose poverty complicates asthma or diabetes, or who get hit by a drunk driver, or who have to keep their mouths closed because their teeth are rotting ought to bear a greater share of the costs of their health care than those of us who are lucky enough to escape such misfortunes? In the rest of the industrialized world, it is assumed that the more equally and widely the burdens of illness are shared, the better off the population as a whole is likely to be. The reason the United States has forty-five million people without coverage is that its health-care policy is in the hands of people who disagree, and who regard health insurance not as the solution but as the problem.

> *"The American health care system, high expenditures and all, is driving innovation for the entire world."*

The U.S. Health Care System Is a Leader in Medical Innovation Despite Its Shortcomings

Tyler Cowen

Tyler Cowen, who is a professor of economics at George Mason University, argues in this viewpoint that however inefficient the U.S. health care system is, it is nevertheless the world leader in medical research. Addressing inequities of access or eliminating waste in the system by moving closer to European models for universal health care would possibly have the unintended consequence of putting U.S. superiority in research and innovation at risk.

As you read, consider the following questions:

1. How many American researchers have won the Nobel Prize in medicine in the past ten years?

2. How does spending for biomedical research in the United States compare with spending in European Union countries? Why is this important?

3. The author suggests that there is a positive relationship between medical innovation and the amount of waste and chaos in the system. Why might this be true?

Advocates of national health insurance cite an apparently devastating fact: the United States spends more of its gross domestic product on medical care than any nation in the world, yet Americans do not live longer than Western Europeans or Japanese. More Americans lack insurance coverage as well. It is no wonder that so many people demand reform.

But the American health care system may be performing better than it seems at first glance. When it comes to medical innovation, the United States is the world leader. In the last ten years [1996–2006], for instance, twelve Nobel Prizes in medicine have gone to American-born scientists working in the United States, three have gone to foreign-born scientists working in the United States, and just seven have gone to researchers outside the country.

A Land of Innovation

The six most important medical innovations of the last twenty-five years, according to a 2001 poll of physicians, were magnetic resonance imaging [MRI] and computed tomography (CT scan); ACE inhibitors, used in the treatment of hypertension and congestive heart failure; balloon angioplasty; statins to lower cholesterol levels; mammography; and coronary artery bypass grafts. Balloon angioplasty came from Europe, four innovations on the list were developed in American hospitals or by American companies (although statins were based on earlier Japanese research), and mammography was first developed in Germany and then improved in the United

States. Even when the initial research is done overseas, the American system leads in converting new ideas into workable commercial technologies.

In real terms, spending on American biomedical research has doubled since 1994. By 2003, spending was up to $94.3 billion (there is no comparable number for Europe), with 57 percent of that coming from private industry. The National Institutes of Health's current annual research budget is $28 billion. All European Union governments, in contrast, spent $3.7 billion in 2000, and since that time, Europe has not narrowed the research and development gap. America spends more on research and development overall and on drugs in particular, even though the United States has a smaller population than the core European Union countries. From 1989 to 2002, four times as much money was invested in private biotechnology companies in America than in Europe.

Dr. Thomas Boehm of Jerini, a biomedical research company in Berlin, titled his article in the *Journal of Medical Marketing* in 2005 "How Can We Explain the American Dominance in Biomedical Research and Development?" Dr. Boehm argues that the research environment in the United States, compared with Europe, is wealthier, more competitive, more meritocratic and more tolerant of waste and chaos. He argues that these features lead to more medical discoveries. About 400,000 European researchers are living in the United States, usually for superior financial compensation and research facilities.

This innovation-rich environment stems from the money spent on American health care and also from the richer and more competitive American universities. The American government could use its size, or use the law, to bargain down health care prices, as many European governments have done. In the short run, this would save money but in the longer run it would cost lives.

Innovation and Reform

Health care reform, which seeks to expand coverage and control spending, contains mixed messages for innovators. Policies that advance reform goals are likely to shift resources away from hospitals, specialists, and expensive procedures and toward areas such as prevention and primary care, where innovation may yield greater health improvements per dollar spent. The size of these effects depends critically on the extent of cost containment achieved. Constraining spending will be politically difficult because it requires that consumers forgo some possible health benefits in return for lower costs. In a climate of cost containment, systematic evaluation of new technology is vital to identify and expand coverage to worthwhile innovations and to assure a fair hearing for innovators.

Jane E. Sisk and Sherry A. Glied,
"Innovation Under Federal Health Care Reform,"
Health Affairs, *Summer 1994.*

Medical innovations improve health and life expectancy in all wealthy countries, not just in the United States. That is one reason American citizens do not live longer. Furthermore, the lucrative United States health care market enhances research and development abroad and not just at home.

The Benefits of Innovation

The gains from medical innovations are high. For instance, increases in life expectancy resulting from better treatment of cardiovascular disease from 1970 to 1990 have been conservatively estimated as bringing benefits worth more than $500 billion a year. And that is just for the United States.

The American system also produces benefits that are hard to find in the numbers. The economist Arnold Kling in his *Crisis of Abundance: Rethinking How We Pay for Health Care* (2006) argues that the expected life span need increase by only about half a year for the extra American health care spending to be cost-effective over a twenty-year period. Given that many Americans walk less and eat less healthy food than most Europeans, the longevity boost from health care in the United States may be real but swamped by the results of poor lifestyle choices. In the meantime, the extra money Americans spend to treat allergy symptoms, pain, depression and discomfort contributes to personal happiness.

Compared with Europe, the American system involves more tests, more procedures and more visits with specialists. Sick people receive more momentary comforts and also the sense that everything possible has been done. This feeling is of value to the family even when the patient does not improve. In contrast, European countries have not created comparably high expectations about the medical process. If we count "giving people what they would want, if they knew it was there" as one measure of medical value, the American system looks better.

American health care has many problems. Health insurance is linked too tightly to employment, and too many people cannot afford insurance. Insurance companies put too much energy into avoiding payments. Personal medical records are kept on paper rather than in accessible electronic fashion. Emergency rooms are not always well suited to serve as last-resort health care for the poor. Most fundamentally, the lack of good measures of health care quality makes it hard to identify and eliminate waste.

These problems should be addressed, but it would be hasty to conclude that the United States should move closer to European health care institutions. The American health care system, high expenditures and all, is driving innovation for the entire world.

Periodical Bibliography

The following articles have been selected to supplement the diverse views presented in this chapter.

Cesar Chelala	"U.S. Health Care Is Bad for Your Health," *San Francisco Chronicle*, January 19, 2009.
Forbes	"Medicare's 'No' on Virtual Colonoscopy Stirs Expert Debate," May 9, 2009.
Kristen Gerencher	"Americans Down on the U.S. Health-Care System," *Market Watch*, July 13, 2008.
Todd Huffman	"The Turnabout for Doctors on Health Care Reform," *Oregon Live*, May 13, 2009.
John Ibbitson	"Why Fixing Health Care Is a Tough Task for Obama," *Globe and Mail America*, May 14, 2009.
Paul Krugman	"Health Care Horror Stories," *New York Times*, April 11, 2008.
Noam N. Levey	"Medicare Trustees Warn of Budget Crisis," *San Francisco Chronicle*, May 13, 2009.
Thomas G. Pretlow	"Our Health Care System Needs a Heart Transplant," *U.S. Catholic*, September 2008.
James H. "Smokey" Shott	"U.S. Health System Needs Tweaking, Not a Comprehensive Overhaul," *Bluefield Daily Telegraph*, May 18, 2009.
Justin Sugg	"Of Numerous Health-Care Plans, None Gets It Right." *Daily Iowan*, May 14, 2009.
Michael van der Galien	"Health Care Costs Are the Elephant in the Room," *PoliGazette*, May 15, 2009.
George F. Will	"Health-Care Horror: The Coming Entitlement Crash," *New York Post*, January 2, 2009.

OPPOSING
VIEWPOINTS®
SERIES

CHAPTER 2

Is Access to Health Care a Moral Issue?

Chapter Preface

In its 2003 report, *Hidden Costs, Value Lost: Uninsurance in America*, the Institute of Medicine explored the economic and social consequences of lack of heath insurance on individuals, families, and communities. The report also outlined benefits that could be realized if health insurance was universally and continually available, and concluded that the dollar value of insuring all Americans was between $65 billion and $130 billion per year. The Institute of Medicine supports universal, continual, and affordable health insurance for all Americans, and makes its case on the basis of economics—that it would be more cost-effective for society to provide affordable health insurance than to leave people to manage on their own. Many voices in the health care debate base their arguments on moral principles rather than economic analysis, however.

For example, President Franklin D. Roosevelt, whose administration during the Great Depression and World War II (1933–45) was known for its major reforms, authored a document called "The Economic Bill of Rights," published in 1943. Roosevelt believed freedom from want to be one of four essential human liberties and defined freedom to include "the right to adequate medical care and the opportunity to achieve and enjoy good health." Later, the United Nations incorporated Roosevelt's notion of a human right to health in the Universal Declaration of Human Rights, a document that has achieved international recognition. Advocates for universal health care who appeal to the idea of a human right to health—for example, the National Health Care for the Homeless Council and the international public health advocacy organization, Partners in Health—are indebted to Franklin Roosevelt, and also to the Universal Declaration of Human Rights, for the moral character of their arguments.

Other voices in the health care debate make moral arguments that are grounded in religious traditions. For example, the late Cardinal Joseph Bernardin (1978–1996) of Chicago once said, "Health care is an essential safeguard of human life and dignity and there is an obligation of society to ensure that every person is able to realize this fundamental right." While Bernardin's language resembled that of the Universal Declaration of Human Rights, it was also rooted in Catholic social teaching and is echoed in Bishop William F. Murphy's July 2009 letter to Congress written on behalf of the U.S. Conference of Catholic Bishops, which concludes that genuine health care reform is a "moral imperative and a vital national obligation."

When Dr. Michael Pontious, an Oklahoma family practice physician and editor of the *Journal of the Oklahoma State Medical Association*, addressed a New Covenant Baptist health care seminar in the summer of 2009, he pointed out that churches have played a historically important role in building the health care infrastructure in the United States. Pontious, who is himself a Baptist, believes that in recent years religious institutions have failed to follow through on a societal commitment to health care that is rooted in Christian ethics. "Because we have abdicated, it's our responsibility to hold our government accountable for trying to fix this problem," he told his listeners. Pontious believes that a publicly available, affordable health insurance option is necessary as a way to introduce competition and keep private health insurance companies honest. He would like to see Christians in the United States play a leadership role in advocating for a system that provides universal access to health care.[1]

An alternative application of Christian teaching to the issue of universal health care can be found in a January 2009 article, "A Christian Prescription for Health-Care Reform," by

1. Marv Knox, "Heath Care System Broken; Christians Should Help Fix It, Speakers Say," *Baptist Standard*, August 10, 2009.

Donald P. Condit. Condit, an orthopedic surgeon, writes from a Catholic perspective. Like Pontious, he recognizes serious strains in the U.S. health care system: rapid and persistent increases in the cost of health care, combined with advancing technology and an aging demographic, have created an unsustainable health care economy. "Approximately 15 percent of Americans lack health insurance and millions are underinsured or struggling with medical bills. Employer-based medical care is disintegrating," he says.

Condit is opposed to the idea of "comprehensive" or "universal" reform such as Pontious proposes if it would involve more government involvement in health care, however. "Our government has a record found wanting in defense of human dignity," he says. He also opposes employer-funded insurance programs. "We respect human dignity by recognizing both a duty to care for the sick and personal responsibility for maintaining our own health," Condit says. He believes that familial and communal bonds provide a stronger moral framework for health care, and that community organizations, unions, and churches would do a better job of providing health insurance at competitive rates. Such organizations would have closer personal connections to the individuals they were covering, and workers would be less susceptible to "double-jeopardy," the economic damage that individuals can experience when illness brings on the loss of employment. "The doctor-patient relationship could be strengthened with less third-party intrusion by government, employer, or insurance carrier."

As these examples demonstrate, moral approaches to the issue of universal health care can encompass a range of perspectives, both religious and philosophical. This chapter showcases a diverse selection of opinions about how moral thought should influence health care policy.

> "For decades ... we have accepted the barbaric consequences of a profit-driven health care system that bullies and denies us basic freedoms."

Access to Health Care Is a Human Right

Helen Redmond

In this viewpoint Helen Redmond, a Licensed Clinical Social Worker and a member of Chicago Single-Payer Action Network (CSPAN), argues that the profit-driven health care system in the United States places an oppressive burden on individuals and families. Mental illnesses among the uninsured often go untreated, or benefits are limited, with the result that some uninsured end up in prison. Substance abuse problems are often uncovered, or coverage has been severely curtailed, while other kinds of illnesses drive the uninsured into credit card debt, or force them to continue working in jobs they do not like in order to hold on to health care benefits. For-profit health care is a form of bondage.

As you read, consider the following questions:

1. The author argues that many mentally ill people who are eligible for health care coverage do not receive it. What are some of the reasons for this?

2. How serious is the shortage of methadone treatment programs? Does the author provide an explanation for the shortage?

3. What is the average amount of credit card debt among the uninsured, according to the author?

At the core of the idea that health care is a human right is freedom. The for-profit health care system in the United States severely restricts our freedom in a number of subtle and not so subtle ways. Instead of freedom there is fear.

The health care crisis impacts every aspect of our lives down to the most seemingly insignificant personal decisions we make. This national bully terrorizes and forces us to live in fear. It determines what is possible and not possible, it crushes hopes and dreams and imprisons people into lives they did not choose. For decades in this country we have accepted the barbaric consequences of a profit-driven health care system that bullies and denies us basic freedoms. Therefore, we are not free.

How does the bully do this? Let me count the ways.

Health Care Terror and the Mentally Ill

Arguably one of the most inhuman consequences of the health care crisis is the predicament of the mentally ill. People with serious mental illness encounter stigma, discrimination and difficulty accessing treatment. Millions of adults and children suffer from a variety of treatable mental health problems: depression, anxiety, schizophrenia, and pervasive developmental disorder. But insurers avoid covering those with a diagnosed mental disability because of the chronic nature of the problem, which means treatment is often needed for years, and medications are expensive. This cuts into profit margins. Moreover, mental illness is not covered on a par with physical illness by most health insurance policies. The number of visits to mental health providers is limited, typically 20 sessions with a therapist per calendar year, and admission to inpatient psychiatric hospitalization is often restricted to fourteen days and not reimbursed at a hundred percent. This discrimination is perfectly legal and even in states where parity laws have been passed coverage is still uneven. A study titled, "Design of Mental Health Benefits: Still Unequal After All These Years," found that forty-eight percent of workers in employer-sponsored health plans were subjected to the limiting of inpatient days, caps on outpatient visits, and higher co-payments. Leaders in the field of mental health have made the case over and over again that treatment must be both affordable and open-ended because mental illnesses don't respond to rigid timetables.

The barriers for those with insurance coverage are numerous, but for the mentally ill who are uninsured they are almost insurmountable. In major cities, streets and shelters are full of mentally ill people who are not receiving any type of treatment. Most qualify for Medicaid. The problem is actually getting Medicaid coverage. For people with a serious and persistent mental illness—especially the homeless—to negotiate the system and gather all the information needed to apply is almost impossible. They need proof of homelessness and income, a birth certificate, photo identification, copies of bills and a mandatory interview with a case worker. Good luck. The consequence is hundreds of thousands of mentally ill are eligible for coverage but don't get it. Instead, they wander the streets talking to themselves, hearing voices, dirty, hungry, and begging for money.

And they end up in jail. It's shocking: jails and prisons have become de facto psychiatric treatment facilities for the mentally ill. The US Department of Justice reports about sixteen percent of inmates—more than 300,000 people—[have mental illnesses]. One study found that Los Angeles County Jail and Rikers Island in New York City each held more people with mental illness than the largest psychiatric inpatient facility in the United States. In fact, Los Angeles County Jail, to its shame, has become the largest mental health care institution (if you can call a penal institution such a thing) in the country. The jail treats 3,200 seriously mentally ill prisoners every day! For many, it's the first time they've ever received treatment, and some inmates improve quickly. But once they are dumped back on the streets without structure, access to counselors, and medication, they deteriorate. Homeless, delusional, and out of control, they are inevitably rearrested for behaviors related to their untreated mental illness.

The mentally ill are not free.

Health Care Terror and the Addicted

Those with addictions are similarly discriminated against. Addictions to alcohol, opiates, crack/cocaine, and prescription drugs are mental health problems that need ongoing treatment. Here again, insurers restrict benefits to save money. Inpatient treatment used to be twenty-one days; now it has been cut in half to ten, and some plans provide even fewer days. Outpatient treatment is typically twenty visits with a therapist per calendar year. For people struggling with a long-standing addiction, twenty sessions is a cruel joke.

The shortage of treatment slots results in millions being denied care. According to the Illinois Alcohol and Drug Dependence Association, in 2004, 1.5 million Illinois residents didn't receive treatment because they couldn't afford it. A report by Join Together, a national resource center, reported that in San Francisco, 1,500 drug and alcohol users were shut out of treatment daily.

Coverage Matters

Uninsurance at the community level is associated with financial instability for health care providers and institutions, reduced hospital services and capacity, and significant cuts in public health programs, which may diminish access to certain types of care for all residents, even those who have coverage.

Institute of Medicine, Insuring America's Health,
National Academy Press, 2004.

Methadone maintenance, despite being the most successful, and cost-effective treatment for heroin addiction, is in seriously short supply. There are roughly 810,000 heroin addicts and only 170,000 funded methadone treatment slots. The wait lists are legendary, at one point in the state of Washington the wait was up to 18 months, and in New York there were 8,000 people on a waiting list! In Columbus, Ohio, it took Heather Bara eighteen months to get into a methadone program. While waiting, she overdosed twice.

The drug addicted are not free.

The Danger of Bankruptcy

The health care medical industrial complex is an enormous part of the economy and health care spending now accounts for 16 percent of Gross Domestic Product. Half of all personal bankruptcies are caused by illness or medical bills. The number of medical bankruptcies has increased by 2,200 percent since 1981. Have you ever tried to pay back half a million dollars for an unplanned and uninsured "stay" in an intensive care unit? Shit-out-[of-]luck stroke that I had! But even those with insurance have good reason to fear bankruptcy. Just ask the parents of three-year-old Elly Bachman. She was bitten by a snake. The treatment for the bite—including antivenins and several surgeries to save the leg—cost the family nearly $91,000 after insurance paid out. The hospital, in a moment of charity, waived $49,000. Now the Bachmans owe $42,000. They have set up a website. Go to www.ellysnakebitefund.org to make a donation.

The Bachmans are not free.

Credit/debit cards are increasingly used to pay for co-pays, deductibles, medication, medical supplies, routine exams, and diagnostic testing. An MRI costs over one thousand dollars. If you had a suspicious mass in your brain would you put the MRI on your Visa? MRI one-thousand dollars, hospital charges two-thousand dollars, medication three-hundred dollars. Peace of mind that you don't have a malignant brain tumor: PRICE-LESS! Except there is a price. Many hospitals and clinics prominently display their price list like a menu, as if purchasing health care was akin to going to a restaurant: I'll have the mammogram, well done, please.

A study titled *Borrowing to Stay Healthy: How Credit Card Debt Is Related to Medical Expenses* by Cindy Zeldin and Mark Rukaivan (www.accessproject.org), illustrates how deeply indebted millions of people are due to the high cost of health care. The cost of health insurance continues to outpace inflation and wage growth. In other words, health care is more expensive and there is less money to pay for it. Now, about 29 million adults have medical debt and—no surprise here—debt acts as a disincentive to filling prescriptions, and following through with recommended treatments or diagnostic tests. If there were still debtors prisons 29 million people would be in them.

According to the study, the uninsured have an average credit card debt of $14,512 in medical debt and those with insurance have $10,973. The average credit card debt for those in households with children was $12,840, and [for] those without children $10,669. The numbers can't convey the reality of what debt costs families and individuals in terms of quality of life. It means parents can't buy their children other things: a computer, trumpet lessons, Hannah Montana tickets (if you could even get them), or a week in Disneyland. For adults, it means a working life dedicated to paying off medical debt instead of buying a home or taking vacations.

Using Plastic to Pay for Care

The credit card industry has recognized the growing market for patient out-of-pocket-costs and has designed "medical credit cards" specifically for medical expenses. Business is good. In 2001, patients charged $19.5 billion in health care services to Visa cards. Highmark Inc., a health insurer in Pennsylvania, offers a "Health Care Gift Card." The card costs $4.95 (plus shipping and handling), and can be loaded with as little as $25 to as much as $5,000. Now you can give your partner that colonoscopy the proctologist recommended. Or buy yourself that brain shunt for your birthday. Oops, I don't think $5,000 will cover it. Put the outstanding balance on another credit card.

We are not free.

Medical debt is related to another crisis in this country: the mortgage crisis. Another finding in the study by Zeldin and Rukaivan is this: among those households that refinanced their homes or took out a second mortgage, [sixty percent] paid down credit cards with the money. A recent story in the *Chicago Reporter* illustrated the connection between the two. Edward and Thaida Booker bought a home in 2001 with a loan carrying a 6.2 percent interest rate. She was diagnosed with cervical cancer a couple years later and they had to refinance their mortgage at a higher interest rate to access some of the equity to pay off unexpected medical bills. Thaida died, and without her income Mr. Booker was on his own to pay a mortgage that had gone from $800 a month to $1,425. The problem is Booker is retired and his pension and disability payments can't cover the new amount. With help from a housing counselor he was able to negotiate new terms with his lender, but still has to rent out a room in the house and work side jobs to make the mortgage payment.

Edward Booker is not free.

Health Care and Employment

Have you ever stayed in a job that you hated because of the health insurance and [because] you or a family member had a health condition that required frequent doctor visits, labs, and expensive medication? It's called job lock. An article in *BusinessWeek* titled "Held Hostage by Health Care—Fear of Losing Coverage Keeps People at Jobs Where They're Not Their Most Productive" exposes an aspect of the health care crisis that has been little discussed. Workers are chained to jobs for one reason; the employers' health insurance. The article alleges there is "[a] health care refugee in every office." I would wager there are millions of Americans who are desperate to leave their jobs but without coverage, medical bankruptcy and/or a health emergency make the risk of quitting impossible. So we put up with the boredom and abuse (and think we are "lucky" to have medical benefits), but if insurance wasn't tied to employment we could tell our boss to "Take this job and shove it!"

Kathryn Holmes Johnson is a health care refugee profiled in the *BusinessWeek* article. For a decade Johnson wanted to leave her job to find one that she really loved, but her husband and two children all have asthma and other health problems. The entire family is covered through her medical plan. The $2,000 a year in co-payments for the family's prescription drugs would have turned into $85,000 without insurance. When she considered changing jobs, the critical factor was the prescription drug coverage that a new employer would offer.

She wondered, "In what other country would that be the deciding factor?" Only in America—a nation of health care hostages.

We are not free.

> *"All legitimate rights have one thing in common: they are rights to action, not to rewards from other people."*

Health Care Is Not a Right

Leonard Peikoff

Leonard Peikoff is the founder of the Ayn Rand Institute and the author of Objectivism: The Philosophy of Ayn Rand. *In this viewpoint he argues that treating health care as a human right requires that services that belong to some people—doctors—are given for free to others. Health care can only be treated as a right through a violation of personal rights of doctors.*

As you read, consider the following questions:

1. What does the author mean when he says that all legitimate rights are rights to action?

2. Does the author believe that most people can afford health care? Why or why not?

3. What moral principle does the author argue doctors must assert?

Most people who oppose socialized medicine do so on the grounds that it is moral and well-intentioned, but impractical; i.e., it is a noble idea—which just somehow does not work. I do not agree that socialized medicine is moral and well-intentioned, but impractical. Of course, it *is* impractical—it does *not* work—but I hold that it is impractical *because* it is immoral. This is not a case of noble in theory but a failure in practice; it is a case of vicious in theory and *therefore* a disaster in practice. I want to focus on the moral issue at stake. So long as people believe that socialized medicine is a noble plan, there is no way to fight it. You cannot stop a noble plan—not if it really is noble. The only way you can defeat it is to unmask it—to show that it is the very opposite of noble. Then at least you have a fighting chance.

What is morality in this context? The American concept of it is officially stated in the Declaration of Independence. It upholds man's unalienable, individual *rights*. The term "rights," note, is a moral (not just a political) term; it tells us that a certain course of behavior is right, sanctioned, proper, a prerogative to be respected by others, not interfered with—and that anyone who violates a man's rights is: wrong, morally wrong, unsanctioned, evil.

Now our only rights, the American viewpoint continues, are the rights to life, liberty, property, and the pursuit of happiness. That's all. According to the Founding Fathers, we are not born with a right to a trip to Disneyland, or a meal at McDonald's, or a kidney dialysis (nor with the 18th-century equivalent of these things). We have certain specific rights—and only these.

Why *only* these? Observe that all legitimate rights have one thing in common: they are rights to action, not to rewards from other people. The American rights impose no obligations on other people, merely the negative obligation to leave you alone. The system guarantees you the chance to work for what you want—not to be given it without effort by somebody else.

The right to life, e.g., does not mean that your neighbors have to feed and clothe you; it means you have the right to earn your food and clothes yourself, if necessary by a hard struggle, and that no one can forcibly stop your struggle for these things or steal them from you if and when you have achieved them. In other words: you have the right to act, and to keep the results of your actions, the products you make, to keep them or to trade them with others, if you wish. But you have no right to the actions or products of others, except on terms to which they voluntarily agree.

To take one more example: the right to the pursuit of happiness is precisely that: the right, to the *pursuit*—to a certain type of action on your part and its result—not to any guarantee that other people will make you happy or even try to do so. Otherwise, there would be no liberty in the country: if your mere desire for something, anything, imposes a duty on other people to satisfy you, then they have no choice in their lives, no say in what they do, they have no liberty, they cannot pursue *their* happiness. Your "right" to happiness at their expense means that they become rightless serfs, i.e., your slaves. Your right to *anything* at others' expense means that they become rightless.

That is why the U.S. system defines rights as it does, strictly as the rights to action. This was the approach that made the U.S. the first truly free country in all world history—and, soon afterwards, as a result, the greatest country in history, the richest and the most powerful. It became the most powerful because its view of rights made it the most moral. It was the country of individualism and personal independence.

Today, however, we are seeing the rise of principled *immorality* in this country. We are seeing a total abandonment by the intellectuals and the politicians of the moral principles on which the U.S. was founded. We are seeing the complete destruction of the concept of rights. The original American idea has been virtually wiped out, ignored as if it had never existed. The rule now is for politicians to ignore and violate men's actual rights, while arguing about a whole list of rights never dreamed of in this country's founding documents—rights which require no earning, no effort, no action at all on the part of the recipient.

You are entitled to something, the politicians say, simply because it exists and you want or need it—period. You are entitled to be given it by the government. Where does the government get it from? What does the government have to do to private citizens—to their individual rights—to their *real* rights—in order to carry out the promise of showering free services on the people?

The answers are obvious. The newfangled rights wipe out real rights—and turn the people who actually create the goods and services involved into servants of the state. The Russians tried this exact system for many decades. Unfortunately, we have not learned from their experience. Yet the meaning of socialism is clearly evident in any field at all—you don't need to think of health care as a special case; it is just as apparent if the government were to proclaim a universal right to food, or to a vacation, or to a haircut. I mean: a right in the new sense: not that you are free to earn these things by your own effort and trade, but that you have a moral claim to be given these things free of charge, with no action on your part, simply as handouts from a benevolent government.

How would these alleged new rights be fulfilled? Take the simplest case: you are born with a moral right to hair care, let us say, provided by a loving government free of charge to all who want or need it. What would happen under such a moral theory?

Haircuts are free, like the air we breathe, so some people show up every day for an expensive new styling, the government pays out more and more, barbers revel in their huge new incomes, and the profession starts to grow ravenously, bald men start to come in droves for free hair implantations, a school of fancy, specialized eyebrow pluckers develops—it's all free, the government pays. The dishonest barbers are having a field day, of course—but so are the honest ones; they are working and spending like mad, trying to give every customer his heart's desire, which is a millionaire's worth of special hair care and services—the government starts to scream, the budget is out of control. Suddenly directives erupt: we must limit the number of barbers, we must limit the time spent on haircuts, we must limit the permissible type of hair styles; bureaucrats begin to split hairs about how many hairs a barber should be allowed to split. A new computerized office of records filled with inspectors and red tape shoots up; some barbers, it seems, are still getting too rich, they must be getting more than their fair share of the national hair, so barbers have to start applying for Certificates of Need in order to buy razors, while peer review boards are established to assess every stylist's work, both the dishonest and the overly honest alike, to make sure that no one is too bad or too good or too busy or too unbusy. Etc. In the end, there are lines of wretched customers waiting for their chance to be routinely scalped by bored, hog-tied haircutters, some of whom remember dreamily the old days when somehow everything was so much better.

Do you think the situation would be improved by having hair-care cooperatives organized by the government?—having them engage in managed competition, managed by the government, in order to buy haircut insurance from companies controlled by the government?

If this is what would happen under government-managed hair care, what else can possibly happen—it is already starting to happen—under the idea of *health* care as a right? Health care in the modern world is a complex, scientific, technological service. How can anybody be born with a right to such a thing?

Under the American system you have a right to health care if you can pay for it, i.e., if you can earn it by your own action and effort. But nobody has the right to the services of any professional individual or group simply because he wants them and desperately needs them. The very fact that he needs these services so desperately is the proof that he had better respect the freedom, the integrity, and the rights of the people who provide them.

You have a right to work, not to rob others of the fruits of their work, not to turn others into sacrificial, rightless animals laboring to fulfill your needs.

Some of you may ask here: But can people afford health care on their own? Even leaving aside the present government-inflated medical prices, the answer is: Certainly people can afford it. Where do you think the money is coming from *right now* to pay for it all—where does the government get its fabled unlimited money? Government is not a productive organization; it has no source of wealth other than confiscation of the citizens' wealth, through taxation, deficit financing or the like.

But, you may say, isn't it the "rich" who are really paying the costs of medical care now—the rich, not the broad bulk of the people? As has been proved time and again, there are not enough rich anywhere to make a dent in the government's costs; it is the vast middle class in the U.S. that is the only source of the kind of money that national programs like government health care require. A simple example of this is the fact that all of these new programs rest squarely on the backs not of Big Business, but of small businessmen who are struggling in today's economy merely to stay alive and in existence. Under any socialized regime, it is the "little people" who do most of the paying for it—under the senseless pretext that "the people" can't afford such and such, so the government must take over. If the people of a country truly couldn't afford a certain service—as e.g. in Somalia—neither, for that very reason, could any government in that country afford it, either.

Some people can't afford medical care in the U.S. But they are necessarily a small minority in a free or even semi-free country. If they were the majority, the country would be an utter bankrupt and could not even think of a national medical program. As to this small minority, in a free country they have to rely solely on private, voluntary charity. Yes, charity, the kindness of the doctors or of the better off—charity, not right, i.e. not their right to the lives or work of others. And such charity, I may say, was always forthcoming in the past in America. The advocates of Medicaid and Medicare under LBJ did not claim that the poor or old in the '60's got bad care; they claimed that it was an affront for anyone to have to depend on charity.

But the fact is: You don't abolish charity by calling it something else. If a person is getting health care for *nothing*, simply because he is breathing, he is still getting charity, whether or not any politician, lobbyist or activist calls it a "right." To call it a Right when the recipient did not earn it is merely to compound the evil. It is charity still—though now extorted by criminal tactics of force, while hiding under a dishonest name.

As with any good or service that is provided by some specific group . . . if you try to make its possession by all a right, you thereby enslave the providers of the service, wreck the service, and end up depriving the very consumers you are supposed to be helping. To call "medical care" a right will merely enslave the doctors and thus destroy the quality of medical care in this country, as socialized medicine has done around the world, wherever it has been tried, including Canada (I was born in Canada and I know a bit about that system firsthand).

I would like to clarify the point about socialized medicine enslaving the doctors. Let me quote here from an article I wrote a few years ago: "Medicine: The Death of a Profession."

In medicine, above all, the mind must be left free. Medical treatment involves countless variables and options that must be taken into account, weighed, and summed up by the doctor's mind and subconscious. Your life depends on the private, inner essence of the doctor's function: it depends on the input that enters his brain, and on the processing such input receives from him. What is being thrust now into the equation? It is not only objective medical facts any longer. Today, in one form or another, the following also has to enter that brain: 'The DRG administrator [in effect, the hospital or HMO man trying to control costs] will raise hell if I operate, but the malpractice attorney will have a field day if I don't—and my rival down the street, who heads the local PRO [peer review organization], favors a CAT scan in these cases, I can't afford to antagonize him, but the CON boys disagree and they won't authorize a CAT scanner for our hospital—and besides the FDA prohibits the drug I should be prescribing, even though it is widely used in Europe, and the IRS might not allow the patient a tax deduction for it, anyhow, and I can't get a specialist's advice because the latest Medicare rules prohibit a consultation with this diagnosis, and maybe I shouldn't even take this patient, he's so sick—after all, some doctors are manipulating their slate of patients, accept only the healthiest ones, so their average costs are coming in lower than mine, and it looks bad for my staff privileges." Would you like your case to be treated this way—by a doctor who takes into account your objective medical needs *and* the contradictory, unintelligible demands of some ninety different state and Federal government agencies? If you were a doctor could you comply with all of it? Could you plan or work around or deal with the unknowable? But how could you not? Those agencies are real and they are rapidly gaining total power over you and your mind and your patients.

In this kind of nightmare world, if and when it takes hold fully, thought is helpless; no one can decide by rational means what to do. A doctor either obeys the loudest authority—*or* he tries to sneak by unnoticed, bootlegging some good health care occasionally *or*, as so many are doing now, he simply gives up and quits the field. (*The Voice of Reason: Essays in Objectivist Thought*, NAL Books, 1988, pp. 306–307)

Any mandatory and comprehensive plan will finish off quality medicine in this country—because it will finish off the medical profession. It will deliver doctors bound hands and feet to the mercies of the bureaucracy.

The only hope—for the doctors, for their patients, for all of us—is for the doctors to assert a *moral* principle. I mean: to assert their own personal individual rights—their real rights in this issue—their right to their lives, their liberty, their property, *their* pursuit of happiness. The Declaration of Independence applies to the medical profession too. We must reject the idea that doctors are slaves destined to serve others at the behest of the state.

Doctors, Ayn Rand wrote, are not servants of their patients. They are "traders, like everyone else in a free society, and they should bear that title proudly, considering the crucial importance of the services they offer."

The battle against socialized medicine depends on the doctors speaking out against it—not only on practical grounds, but, first of all, on moral grounds. The doctors must defend themselves and their own interests as a matter of solemn justice, upholding a moral principle, the first moral principle: self-preservation.

*"It's ironic but true: Only by abandon-
ing attempts to provide healthcare as a
'right' that's paid for largely by others
will we enjoy surer access to it."*

Treating Health Care as a Human Right Would Increase Health Care Costs

Donald J. Boudreaux

*In this viewpoint, Donald Boudreaux, chairman of the Econom-
ics Department at George Mason University, argues that it would
make poor economic sense to treat access to health care as a human right. With health care freely available, individuals would
use more health care than they actually needed, driving up the
cost of care, and creating a very inefficient system. Allowing
market forces to drive the cost of health care leads to more efficient use of resources and ensures that greater numbers of people
enjoy access to health care.*

As you read, consider the following questions:

1. What does the author say would be the result if the government tried to supply food as a universally available
   right?

2. Do you think people would tend to overuse health care in the same way they might overuse food?

3. How does the author feel about the efficiency of the Medicare and Medicaid programs?

Everyone complains about the rising cost of healthcare. And now is the season when politicians and pundits propose solutions. Unfortunately, too many of these proposals spring from the wrongheaded notion that healthcare is, as a recent *New York Times* letter-writer asserted, "a human right and a universal entitlement."

Sounds noble. But not everything that is highly desirable is a right. Most rights simply oblige us to respect one another's freedoms; they do not oblige us to pay for others to exercise these freedoms. Respecting rights such as freedom of speech and of worship does not impose huge demands upon taxpayers.

Health Care Is a Scarce Resource

Healthcare, although highly desirable, differs fundamentally from these rights. Because providing healthcare takes scarce resources, offering it free at the point of delivery would raise its cost and reduce its availability.

To see why, imagine if government tried to supply food as a universally available "right."

To satisfy this right, government would raise taxes to meet all anticipated food needs. Store shelves across the land would then be stocked. Citizens would have the right to enter these storehouses to get "free" food.

Does anyone believe that such a system would effectively supply food? It's clear that with free access to food, too many people would take too much food, leaving many others with no food at all. Government would soon realize that food storehouses are emptying faster than expected. In response, it might hike taxes even higher to produce more food—raising the price that society pays for nutrition.

Stocking stores with more food, though, won't solve the problem. With food free at the point of delivery, consumers would take all that they can carry. People would quickly learn that if they don't grab as much food as possible today, the store might run out of the foods that their families need tomorrow. This creates a vicious cycle of moral hazard that unwittingly pits neighbor against neighbor.

Eventually, to avoid spending impossibly large chunks of society's resources producing food, government would start restricting access to it. Bureaucrats would enforce rations, such as "two gallons of milk per family per week." There might be exceptions for those with special needs, but most of us would be allowed to take only those foods that officials decide we need.

Food would be a universal entitlement in name only. In practice, it would be strictly limited by government rules.

Of course, by keeping what food it does supply "free," government might ensure that at least basic foodstuffs are available to everyone as a right. And maybe this is the sort of outcome that universal healthcare advocates have in mind: Only essential care is a right to be enjoyed by everyone free of charge.

The problem is that notions of "essential care" are vague. Is medical care essential if doctors say it might improve by 50 percent an 80-year-old's chances of living an additional year? What about care that improves by 10 percent a 25-year-old's chances of living an additional 50 years? Such questions are wickedly difficult to answer.

A Demand That Cannot Be Met

Despite these difficulties, many Americans demand that government do more to guarantee access to healthcare. Although their concern is understandable, those who make such de-

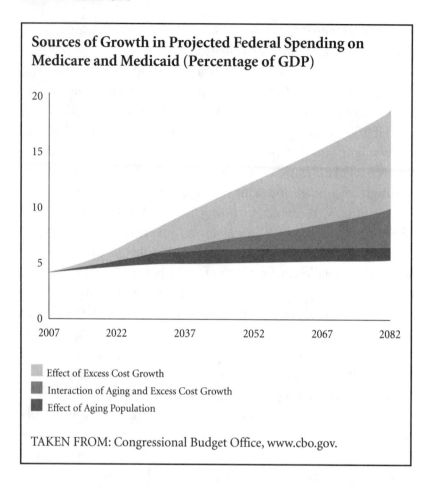

Sources of Growth in Projected Federal Spending on Medicare and Medicaid (Percentage of GDP)

Effect of Excess Cost Growth

Interaction of Aging and Excess Cost Growth

Effect of Aging Population

TAKEN FROM: Congressional Budget Office, www.cbo.gov.

mands forget that government intervention itself is a major cause of today's high and rising healthcare costs. Indeed, this intervention has created a situation akin to what would happen if government supplied our food for "free."

Medicare, Medicaid, and tax-deductibility of employer-provided health insurance created a system in which patients at the point of delivery now pay only a small fraction of their medical bills out of pocket.

This situation leads to monstrously inefficient consumption of healthcare. Some people consume too much, while many others with more pressing needs do without.

Because the wasteful consumption caused by heavily subsidized access drives up healthcare costs, taxpayers must pay more and more to fund Medicare and Medicaid, while private insurers must continually raise premiums. The sad and perverse result is that increasing numbers of people go without health insurance.

The solution is less, not more, government involvement in healthcare. Market forces have consistently lowered the cost and improved the quality and accessibility of food—which is at least as important to human survival as is healthcare. There's no reason markets can't do the same for healthcare.

It's ironic but true: Only by abandoning attempts to provide healthcare as a "right" that's paid for largely by others will we enjoy surer access to it.

> "Health care is a fundamental human right that should be available to all people regardless of their economic resources."

Treating Health Care as a Human Right Would Reduce Health Care Costs

Gary Dorrien

Gary Dorrien, professor of religion at Columbia University and the Reinhold Niebuhr Professor of Social Ethics at Union Theological Seminary, argues that health care is a basic human right. He describes the single–payer health care system as an improvement on the Medicare system—health care for everyone. Dorrien believes that the private insurance companies hold too much power.

As you read, consider the following questions:

1. According to the author, the single–payer health care system would be similar to the health care systems in which countries?

2. As stated in the viewpoint, how many Americans are left without health coverage?

3. According to Dorrien, what is the "real worry" for the supporters of the current health care system?

Longtime advocates of single-payer insurance like me are thrilled, anxious and deflated simultaneously by the state of the debate on health-care reform. The debate that we wanted has finally come, and it is coming with a legislative rush, but the plan that we wanted is being excluded from consideration. Should we hold out for the real thing, or get behind the best politically possible thing?

I am for doing both: Standing up for single-payer without holding out for it exclusively; supporting a public option without denying its limitations; and hoping that a good public plan will lead eventually to real national health insurance.

The Single-Payer System

Single-payer basically means Medicare for everyone, without the copays and deductibles of the current Medicare system. It is not socialized medicine, as in England or Spain, where doctors and hospitals work for the government. It does not violate the takings clause of the Fifth Amendment, which bars the government from taking private property for public use without appropriate compensation, since it does not nationalize any private firms. The single-payer plan is a system of socialized health insurance similar to that of Canada, Australia and most European nations. Essentially it is an extension and improvement of the Medicare system, in which government pays for care that is managed and delivered in the private sector.

We don't need private health insurance companies. We certainly don't need a system that wastes $450 billion per year in redundant administrative costs and leaves 45 million Americans without health coverage. We could do without a system that excludes people with preexisting medical conditions and limited economic resources. We don't need a system that cherry picks profitable clients and dumps the unprofitably ill in HMOs featuring lousy care and little choice. Businesses and other employers would do much better not having to provide health coverage for their employees, who often end up under-insured. We could do better than a system that ties people fearfully to jobs they want to leave but can't afford to lose be-cause they might lose their health coverage.

The Human Right to Health Care

Health care is a fundamental human right that should be available to all people regardless of their economic resources. A society that takes seriously this elementary principle of so-cial justice does not relegate the poor and underemployed to second-class care or status. The only Western democratic soci-ety that doesn't even try to live up to this principle is the United States. When wealthy and middle-class people have to rely on the same health system as the poor, as they do throughout Europe, they use their political power to make sure it's a decent system.

But single-payer deliverance is not on the agenda for Presi-dent Obama and this Congress. The insurance companies are too powerful and politically aggressive to be retired in one legislative stroke. The House bill that calls for replacing for-profit insurance companies has only 79 cosponsors, and the Senate bill has only one—Bernie Sanders.

Obama rightly urges that significant health-care reform has to happen this year [2009] if it is to happen on his watch. In May he told a town hall meeting in Rio Rancho, New Mexico, that if one were starting from scratch, a single-payer system might be the best option. However, he observed, "the only problem is that we're not starting from scratch." The sys-tem that we have comprises 14 percent of the nation's gross domestic product. Reinventing something that big and politically connected has no chance of happening this year.

The best we can hope for this year is a public Medicare-like option that competes with private plans. This reform would save only 15 percent of the $350 billion insurance overhead costs that converting to single-payer would achieve. Most versions currently being touted would not get everyone covered, though Obama suggested recently that he might be open to changing his position on requiring all Americans to have health coverage. In any case, even the better proposals along this line, like the one that Senator Ted Kennedy has championed for years, would not get us close to equality in health care. But a strong reform bill would offer an important alternative to private health insurance that might pave the way to real national health insurance.

The Possibility of a Public Plan

The insurance companies are gearing up to prevent a public plan because they don't want to compete with one. The American Medical Association doesn't want one either—which preserves its bad-smelling record in this area. The AMA was against Medicare, it has opposed every previous proposal for universal coverage, and today it is against providing a public option even for people lacking the economic means or opportunity to buy health insurance.

Princeton economist and *New York Times* columnist Paul Krugman is almost right in contending that the crucial either/or of the battle over health care is whether reform delivers a public option. But Krugman's point needs to be put more precisely. The acid test is not whether reform delivers a public plan, but whether it delivers a good one. A good public plan would be open to all individuals and employers that want to join. It would allow members to choose their own doctors. It would eliminate high deductibles. It would allow members to negotiate reimbursement rates and drug prices.

The government would run it. And it would be backed up by tough cost controls and a requirement that all Americans have health coverage.

A bad public plan, however, would be worse than getting nothing. A plan that isn't open to everyone or that prevents choice or negotiation would be a plan designed to fail. It would take the pressure off private companies to do something about the uninsured and underinsured without solving the problem. It would be like Medicaid—poorly funded and managed because its beneficiaries lack political power. The failure of a designed-for-failure plan would kill the cause of real national health insurance for another 16 years. Some insurance industry leaders, having figured this out, are ready to indulge a bad plan. The political task for health-care reformers is to create and push through a public plan worth having.

Opponents' Concerns

In this phase of the debate, political and industry opposition to health-care reform is mostly warning that a public option means socialized medicine. A fair amount of time has to be spent repeating over and over that single-payer is not socialized medicine, and a public option among private competitors is even farther from it. But we are approaching the point where opponents of health-care reform will start to stress the opposite concern. Their concern is not that a government program won't work. The real worry, for all who want to keep the present system, is that a government program will work too well.

Overwhelming majorities in blue and red states alike would love to dump their policies containing high deductibles and health exclusions. A public plan could be a magnet for health-care workers that got into this business to serve human needs, not to be cogs in a profit machine. If that happens, opponents will have been right about one important point. Mere reform could lead to the real thing, a single-payer system where substantial savings and equality are achievable. Medicare's average overhad cost is 3 percent, and provincial single-payer plans in Canada average 1 percent. HMOs range between 15 and 25 percent. If we create a public plan that people want to join, we may well go the rest of the way too.

> "The prospect of government-funded universal health care ... is another example of America's departure from its strong Judeo-Christian roots and its love affair with socialism."

Universal Health Care Is Unbiblical

Mark H. Creech

In this viewpoint Mark Creech, the executive director of Christian Action League of North Carolina, argues that universal heath care proposals are unbiblical because they propose redistributing wealth to equalize access to health care. The Bible sees creativity and productivity as essential qualities of human beings, who are made in God's image. It is immoral to create a system that redistributes economic goods, since it deprives individuals of the ability to benefit from their own creative and productive work. Any plan that fosters dependence on government is not only dangerous but also immoral.

As you read, consider the following questions:

1. The author recognizes that most Americans favor federal health insurance. Why does he believe they reached this erroneous conclusion?

Mark H. Creech, "Universal Health Care: Unbiblical Socialism," *WorldNetDaily.com*, March 17, 2007. © 2009. Reproduced by permission.

2. Why are socialistic endeavors inherently immoral, according to the author?

3. In what ways does the author believe that liberty and justice would be diminished by a federally funded plan for universal health care?

Universal health care, or government-funded health insurance, is a major issue early on in the [2008] presidential campaign. North Carolina's former senator, John Edwards, has been stumping for it in his platform for president. Hillary Rodham Clinton, also a candidate for the presidency, has been pushing for it as far back as when her husband, Bill Clinton, first became president. It's also been a burning issue for state governments such as California and Massachusetts. Even a House Select Committee, in a state as conservative as North Carolina, has been studying the California and Massachusetts models of legislation with the prospect of making an attempt at providing universal health care for the Tar Heel State.

America Has Lost Its Way

The prospect of government-funded universal health care, however, is another example of America's departure from its strong Judeo-Christian roots and its love affair with socialism. Most Americans are completely unfamiliar with what the Bible teaches about economics. And progressive churches have, unfortunately, dominated the scene by espousing a form of economics that is essentially socialistic principles with a religious veneer. One might even argue the church's loss of influence today is due in part to its support and advancement of the welfare state, which by government pre-emption has siphoned away the church's energy and resources for charitable purposes.

While a recent *New York Times*/CBS News Poll finds a majority of Americans now say the federal government should provide health insurance to every American, there are strong indications that many who declare their support for government-funded universal heath care fail to understand what it would entail. The poll found "[s]ixty percent, including 62 percent of independents and 46 percent of Republicans, said they would be willing to pay more in taxes. . . . Half said they would be willing to pay as much as $500 a year more." But even if every person currently paying taxes were willing to pay an extra $500 a year, that wouldn't begin to cover the great costs involved in such a program.

The Bible teaches [that] God is a creative and productive being and [that] man, who is made in His image, was created for the same. Economic systems that perpetuate or construct dependence or reward sloth strike at the very heart of what it means to be human. Thus, the apostle Paul admonished the Thessalonians: "For even when we were with you, this we commanded you, that if any would not work, neither should he eat." (II Thessalonians 3:10) Certainly, those who cannot provide for themselves, despite every effort they can summon, should be helped in the form of charity. Nevertheless, the Scriptures teach that ingenuity and industry are what should be rewarded, while laziness or failure to provide a service the public needs should go unrewarded.

What is inherently immoral about socialistic endeavors is the effort to equalize economic conditions by forcibly redistributing wealth. To get this done, the right to private property, which God gives in the eighth commandment of the Decalogue, is violated. And charity, which according to the Scriptures is supposed to spring willingly from the heart, is instead coerced. Therefore, the image of God in man—his creativity and productivity—is suppressed, while those who are indolent prosper.

What is more, socialistic principles fail to take into account man's depravity—his fall away from God and into sin. The socialist contends if man's environment is changed, he will change. He'll be better to his neighbor. It discounts man's

What Jesus Would Do?

One of the things I find frustrating about my fellow Catholics is that more and more of them seem to think that universal health care is not only a good idea, but is what Christ would want, and is the most fair, just, equitable way of making sure that everybody gets adequate health care. . . . Sadly, there is evidence to the contrary.

Erin Manning, "The Push for Universal Health Care,"
February 6, 2009. www.redcardigan.blogspot.com.

need for redemption in Christ and contends that if all have an equal share, then there is less reason to war and steal, etc. But the fact is socialistic principles change nothing about human nature and only concentrates economic power in the hands of a few sinful individuals who are more able to exploit the public.

The Government Should Not Pay for Health Care

Sven Larson, a policy analyst for the John William Pope Civitas Institute, notes all the ways these negatives would play out in a government-funded universal health care system, which is simply a form of socialized medicine.

- It would outlaw private health insurance and give government bureaucrats the exclusive right to set reimbursement rates for physicians, clinics and hospitals. This would not only create supply shortages, but would also likely produce a black market health-care system.

- It would transform the state into the sole purchaser of medical drugs and equipment, hampering cost containment and inviting corruption.

- It would destroy professional freedom for medical professionals. The government would be the sole determiner of the number of medical professionals that could work.

- It would of necessity cap health spending. According to data from the Bureau of Economic Analysis, American health providers increase medical technology by 7 percent per year. Such increases are necessary if new technology is to make its way into hospitals and clinics. If the cap for a government-funded universal health-care system like the one proposed in California had been enacted nationwide in 1960, the cumulative effect would have been to lower current technological standards in hospitals to 1982 levels. One can already see how liberty and justice, which are unalienable rights— God-given rights—are significantly diminished by such a proposal.

Most importantly, since a government-funded universal health-care system would come at a heavy financial burden to the state, one could only imagine how, over time, it would affect right-to-life issues. It most certainly would make abortion and euthanasia readily available. Children with gestational issues of retardation, spina bifida, etc. would likely require abortion. Vulnerable patients such as the chronically ill, disabled or elderly would be allowed to die as in the Terri Schiavo case, or possibly even terminated.

Socialism Always Fails

A government-funded universal health-care system will never provide what its champions promise. Why? Because socialism never provides what it promises and neither can socialized medicine. Instead of providing good health coverage for all, it will ultimately lessen the quality of care for all. As Ludwig von Mises wrote in *Liberalism*, "There is simply no other choice than this: either abstain from interference in the free play of the market, or to delegate the entire management of production and distribution to the government." Is the incompetence of the government in responding to the needs of Hurricane Katrina victims so soon removed from America's memory that it's now willing to place its most personal issues—health-care issues regarding quality of life, life and death—into the hands of a federal bureaucracy that would be approximately three times the size of the Pentagon?

Larson rightly argues, "America has the largest private health insurance market in the world. If allowed, this market could provide universal health care for everyone by meeting every need and every budget." He rightly suggests that one key improvement would be to remove the coverage mandates that states impose on private insurance plans. According to the Council for Affordable Health Insurance, there are 1,843 coverage mandates in the [United States]. "Coverage mandates are sometimes called 'consumer protection,'" says Larson. "But because coverage mandates increase the cost of insurance they actually force many families to go unprotected by shutting them out from affordable health insurance plans." The answer lies in reducing the cost and stimulating competition between the insurance companies, he says.

Whatever the solution, any plan fostering more dependence on the government is not only extremely dangerous, but immoral. Perhaps the country would do well to consider the warning of John Cotton, a founding father of the Massachusetts Bay Colony: "Let all the world learn to give mortal men no greater power than they are content that they shall use, for use it they will."

"An intensive, decade-long push by religious investors has helped contribute to a critical mass in corporate America for sweeping health care reform in the near term."

Universal Health Care Is a Moral Issue for Faith-Based Investors

Interfaith Center on Corporate Responsibility

The Interfaith Center on Corporate Responsibility argues in this viewpoint that during the past decade, faith-based investors have been successful in urging American corporations to embrace principles of universal access to health care, such as ones published by the Institute of Medicine. More than twelve companies, including Starbucks, McDonald's, Target, Lilly, and Aetna, have publicly endorsed principles for health care reform. In addition, shareholder resolutions on universal access to health care have been introduced at the shareholder meetings of many other companies.

"2009: The Year of Health Care Reform?: Faith-Based Investors See Doubling of Related Shareholder Resolutions, Growing Public Support from Corporate America," *Interfaith Center on Corporate Responsibility*, January 14, 2009. © 2009 Interfaith Center on Corporate Responsibility. Reproduced by permission.

As you read, consider the following questions:

1. What is the Interfaith Center on Corporate Responsibility? Who does it represent?

2. What are the five principles of universal health care reform that are listed in this viewpoint?

3. Name three companies that have issued public statements calling for health care reform.

How strong is the impetus from faith-based and other institutional investors for a breakthrough in health care reform in 2009? The Interfaith Center on Corporate Responsibility (ICCR), a coalition of nearly 300 faith-based institutional investors representing over $100 billion in invested capital, reported today [January 14, 2009] that:

• The number of *health care reform shareholder resolutions* at major corporations will rise from 12 in 2008 to 26 in the proxy season for 2009, including such top companies as American Express, Ford, Qualcomm, Stapes, Verizon, Yum! Brands Inc.; and

• The ranks of top U.S. companies publicly embracing principles for health care reform now stands at more than 12, including Starbucks (just this month), McDonald's, Target, Lilly and Aetna. Support for the principles continues to grow; Wal-Mart Stores, Inc., informed religious investors this week of the company's support for the principles. ICCR and other institutional investors detailed how an intensive, decade-long push by religious investors has helped contribute to a critical mass in corporate America for sweeping health care reform in the near term.

Faith-based investors have urged America's corporations to adopt and publicly embrace principles for comprehensive health care reform (such as those based upon principles reported by the Institute of Medicine): (1) health care coverage should be universal; (2) health care coverage should be continuous; (3) health care coverage should be affordable to individuals and families; (4) the health insurance strategy should be affordable and sustainable for society; and (5) health insurance should enhance health and well being by promoting access to high-quality care that is effective, efficient, safe, timely, patient-centered, and equitable.

Rev. David Schilling, program director for human rights, Interfaith Center on Corporate Responsibility: "In the decade since the demise of health care reform efforts in the 1990s, the faith community has continued to call for accessible and affordable health care for all people in a just and compassionate health care system. As long-term institutional investors, members of the Interfaith Center on Corporate Responsibility recognize the economic burden [that] providing health benefits for employees places on American corporations. Faith-based investors believe it is in the economic interest of portfolio companies to ensure that all Americans have access to health care that is affordable and provided equitably."

Sister Barbara Aires, coordinator of corporate responsibility, Sisters of Charity of St. Elizabeth (NJ), said: "Shareholders are important stakeholders in corporations. Our voice is relevant in the debate on health care reform. Health care reform is both a moral and a financial issue. A total of 79 ICCR member institutional investors have signed on to [a] statement saying 'that access to health care is a fundamental human right, benefits society and serves the individual, the common good and employers.' We are encouraged that more than a dozen leading U.S. corporations have joined us in embracing the core principles of needed health care reform."

Cathy Rowan, SRI consultant representing American Baptist Home Mission Society and Trinity Health, said: "Shareholder interests and the public's interests are aligned on the need for comprehensive health care reform. We hope to see corporations present on the day when President Obama signs into law a bill that resolves the lack of access, affordability, quality and accountability in our current health system—and be recognized for the positive role they have played in the public debate."

Laura Shaffer, director of shareholder activities, Nathan Cummings Foundation, said: "As long-term shareholders we want to be sure that the companies we invest in are positioning themselves to shape policy in a way that's beneficial for both society and the bottom line. Corporations that ignore this debate do so at their peril."

Shareholders Are Asking for Reform

In 2007–2008, ICCR members and other institutional investors filed resolutions with a number of companies requesting the boards of directors to adopt principles for comprehensive health care reform, such as those of the Institute of Medicine. Although some companies challenged the resolution at the Securities and Exchange Commission (SEC), the commission eventually told a dozen companies that they must allow shareholders to vote on the proposal to reflect "changing societal views," thereby drawing the corporations deeper into the debate over the future of health care in domestic policy.

In 2009, the ICCR resolution has been filed at (in alphabetical order): 3-M Company; Abbott Laboratories; Altria Group, Inc.; American Express Co.; Apple Computer, Inc. (pending the meeting of filing deadline); Bank of America Corp.; Boeing Company; CBS Corp.; Coca-Cola Enterprises; Direct TV Group, Inc.; Exxon Mobil Corporation; Ford Motor Company; General Motors Corp.; Home Depot, Inc.; Kohl's Corporation (resolution filed and dialogue held); The Kroger Co.; Lowe's Companies, Inc.; Qualcomm, Inc.; Staples, Inc.; Starbucks Corp. (resolution filed and then withdrawn when the company placed principles on its Web site); Target Corp. (resolution filed and dialogue held); United

Technologies Corp.; Verizon Communications, Inc.; Wyeth; Xerox Corporation; and Yum! Brands, Inc.

The 12 resolutions and their outcome in the 2008 shareholder season were as follows (in alphabetical order): Altria (5 percent); Alliant Tech (4 percent); Boeing (6 percent); Comcast (2.4 percent); Ford (4.6 percent); GM (3.7 percent); Lowe's (2.6 percent); Reynolds (.01 percent); UST (3 percent); United Tech (3.8 percent); Wendy's (no vote due to merger with Arby's); and Xcel (8 percent). In addition, primary filers undertook dialogues on this topic with another 20 publicly traded companies.

Companies Are Endorsing Change

As a result of shareholder resolutions and ongoing dialogue, ICCR members have prompted companies to issue public endorsement of health care principles—covering access, quality, affordability, and equitable financing. Companies that have issued such public endorsements include (in alphabetical order):

- Aetna: http://www.aetna.com/about/aoti/ aetna_perspective/uninsured.html

- Bristol-Meyers Squibb: http://www.bms.com/sr/ key_issues/content/data/reform.html

- Cardinal Health: http://www.cardinal.com/us/en/ aboutus/files/pdf/Our%20views%20on%20Healthcare %20Reform%20in%20the%20US%209%203%2008.pdf

- General Electric: http://www/ge.com/news/ our_viewpoints/healthcare_reform.html

- Johnson & Johnson (updated): http://www.jnj.com/wps/ wcm/connect/9e1732804bb7adebabb7efd8109ba68e/us-health-care-reform-principles.pdf?MOD=AJPERES

- Lilly: http://www.lilly.com/about/public_affairs/ positions/#section3

- McDonald's: http:www.mcdonalds.com/usa/good/people/health_care_principles.html

- Merck: http://www.merck.com/about/public_policy/docs/uninsured_and_hcr.pdf

- Pfizer (updated): http://www.pfizer.com/about/public_policy/pfizer_health_reform_principles.jsp

- Starbucks (issued 2009): http://www.starbucks.com/aboutus/Starbucks_Position_on_National_Health_Care_Reform(12-4-08).pdf

- Target: http://:sites.target.com/images/corporate/about/responsibility_report/2008/full_report.pdf

- WellPoint: http://www.bcbs.com/news/plans/wellpoint-unveils-plan-for.html

- Wyeth: http://www.wyeth.com/irj/servlet/prt/portal/prtroot/com.sap.km.cm.docs/wyeth_html/home/aboutwyeth/shared/Docs/uninsured.pdf

Periodical Bibliography

The following articles have been selected to supplement the diverse views presented in this chapter.

Lindsay Barrett   "A Moral Prescription: Faith Community Backs Progressive Proposals for Health," *Center for American Progress*, August 28, 2008.

Paul Farmer   "Health Is a Human Right," *This I Believe: Modern Essays Heard on NPR*, December 21, 2008.

Lee Hieb   "No, Barack, Medical Care Is Not a Right," HumanEvents.com, October 8, 2008.

Nora Jacobson   "A Taxonomy of Dignity: A Grounded Theory Study," *International Health and Human Rights*, February 24, 2009.

Alan Jenkins   "A Human Right to Health," TomPaine.com, October 9, 2007.

Knowledge@Wharton   "Cost-Effective Medical Treatment: Putting an Updated Dollar Value on Human Life," April 30, 2008.

Maggie Mahar   "Is Health Care a 'Right' or a 'Moral Responsibility?'" Alternet, October 2008.

Alicia Ely Yamin   "Will We Take Suffering Seriously? Reflections on What Applying a Human Rights Framework to Health Means and Why We Should Care," *Health and Human Rights: An International Journal* 10, No. 1, 2008.

Lin Zinser and Paul Hsieh   "Moral Health Care Vs. 'Universal Health Care,'" *The Objective Standard: A Journal of Culture and Politics*, Winter 2007–2008.

CHAPTER 3

Does Universal Health Care Work in Other Countries?

Chapter Preface

In the ongoing debate about universal health care, supporters of reform often cite two facts: First, the United States is the only modern, industrialized country that does not provide universal access to health care services; and second, countries that do provide universal access to health care are able to do so at a fraction of the per capita cost of health care in the United States. For example, an article in *Oregon's Future* magazine in 2004 quoted the following figures: Switzerland spends 68 percent as much as the United States on health care, whereas Canada spends 57 percent as much and the United Kingdom spends 44 percent as much.[1] Another measure that is often cited: While the United States spends approximately 15 percent of its gross domestic product on health care, the world average is 7 to 8 percent of GDP. The journal *Health Affairs* estimates that U.S. health care expenditures will rise to 19 percent of GDP by 2016 if the current system of paying for care does not change.

Supporters of universal health care also claim that in spite of spending much less, countries that provide universal health coverage are able to provide better care far more efficiently: a 2007 report on American health care by the Commonwealth Fund found that, when compared to Australia, Canada, Germany, New Zealand, and the United Kingdom on measures like quality, access, efficiency, equity, and healthy lives, the United States consistently ranked last or next to last.[2] Statistics like these are often used to support universal health care as a model that is not only fiscally responsible but also clinically sound.

Opponents of universal health care seldom challenge these arguments on financial grounds. Sometimes their approach is philosophical, as when they label universal health care systems as being, in essence, socialist. For example, addressing health care reform in New Hampshire in July 2007, Republican presidential candidate Rudy Giuliani said, "The American way is not single-payer, government-controlled anything. That's a European way of doing something; that's frankly a socialist way of doing something. . . . When you hear Democrats . . . talk about single-mandated health care, universal health care, what they're talking about is socialized medicine."[3]

Other times, critics of foreign models for achieving universal health care suggest that the quality of care is lower under such systems. In May of 2009 Kim Priestap, a writer for the conservative *American Issues* project, reflected in a blog post on what a government-run health care system would look like: "It is going to have to find ways to make serious cuts in costs," she wrote, "the same way other countries with universal health care find cost savings: through rationing, waiting lists and decreased quality of care." To emphasize her point, Priestap titled her blog post "The Looming Fight Over Health Care Rationing."

Arnold J. Rosoff, a professor of legal studies and business ethics at the Wharton School of the University of Pennsylvania, has identified a set of factors that he says contribute to a country's decision to adopt a universal health care model. In addition to "national character or will" and "public opinion," these include economic strength, history, demographics, politics, and provider infrastructure. Rosoff speculates that the United States, as a result of its unique history, may lack the strong sense of national unity and identity of countries like France and Italy, or of Singapore, which are successful at implementing universal health care systems. In addition, there is in the United States a strong cultural tendency to distrust "big government" and to value personal choice.[4]

The question, "Does universal health care work in other countries?" appears to be a critical one, especially in light of apparent economies of scale that have been achieved in many places. This chapter features a selection of articles that compare the U.S. health care system with the universal health care systems of other countries, and seek to find an answer to that question.

Notes

1. Albert DiPiero, "Universal Problems and Universal Health-care: 6 Countries, 6 Systems," *Oregon's Future*, Fall 2004.
2. Karen Davis, Cathy Schoen, Stephen C. Schoenbaum, Michelle M. Doty, Alyssa L. Holmgren, Jennifer L. Kriss, and Katherine K. Shea, "Mirror, Mirror on the Wall: An International Update on the Comparative Performance of American Health Care," Commonwealth Fund, 2007.
3. Paul Steinhauser, "Giuliani Attacks Democratic Health Plans as 'Socialist,'" *CNN*, July 31, 2007.
4. *Knowledge@Wharton*, "'Harry and Louise,' the Sequel? The Universal Health Care Debate Is Back," June 27, 2007.

> "Living under universal health care has allowed me the freedom to pursue my own happiness. That's surely something that Americans everywhere support."

The Universal Health Care Systems of Other Countries Provide Better Care for Less Money

Karin J. Robinson

Karin J. Robinson, a political consultant and an officer of Democrats Abroad UK, argues in this viewpoint that although there is no single European model for health care reform, Europe does offer several examples of universal health care systems, including Britain's National Health Service, that perform better, and at a lower cost, than the U.S. health care system.

As you read, consider the following questions:

1. The author cites several common criticisms of European health care systems. What are they?

2. What three things do European health care systems have in common, according to the author?

Karin J. Robinson, "Universal Health Care: A Domestic Issue?" *EurObama Blog*, February 5, 2009. Reproduced by permission of the author.

3. The author cites "career reasons" as one factor that leads her to prefer Britain's National Health System to health care options available to her in the United States. What does she mean by "career reasons"?

Despite the recent kerfuffle over Tom Daschle's [Daschle, a former U.S. senator from South Dakota, was President Barack Obama's choice for secretary of health and human services. He withdrew his name because of his failure to report income on his federal tax return] tax problems, I have every hope and expectation that in the coming years, perhaps months, we will start to see a real effort by the [Obama] administration to solve one of the most pressing crises currently facing the USA—rising health care costs and the rapid increase in the [numbers of the] uninsured.

Equally inevitable is that as part of this process we will start to see Conservatives and obstructionists of all sorts piping up to demonise other health care systems that currently have universal coverage. Ranting and raving about the supposed failures of European and Canadian systems seems to be the first club at hand when the opposition tries to beat back any effort at reform. And this view is widely believed by the American public—in fact, my mom told [me] recently that she is very concerned about the quality of health care if America adopts universal cover.

Another Point of View

This is an area where I, and Americans abroad generally, have a useful point of view. After all, many of us have lived under the US health care system and under those supposedly disastrous European systems that folks back home seem to find so worrying. So, from a patient perspective what is better: European style or American style health cover?

Well, the first thing to say is that there is no such thing as "European style" health coverage—countries across the continent all have different delivery models for their universal health care programs. In Britain, somewhat unusually, we have a single institution—the National Health Service (NHS)—that delivers all public sector health care. Other countries, Germany for instance, have an insurance model whereby third party providers offer the health services, but ultimately they are all paid for out of a single pool of taxation.

In fact, virtually the only things the different health systems in Europe have in common with each other are:

1. They are much *cheaper* than the US system.

2. They cover everyone, or almost everyone.

3. They deliver a *better quality* of care.

Here in Britain, for instance, we *spend about 8%* of the country's annual GDP on health care, compared to 15% in the US, and yet the overall health of the population is similar, with perhaps even a slight advantage for the UK. For that 8%, we cover every single person living in the UK (including immigrants, like me).

Thinking About the Real Choices

You will frequently hear people point out that in Britain there are often waiting times for many medical procedures—this is absolutely true and is indeed a serious problem relating to the limited resources of the NHS. They are required to make some difficult decisions about how to spend their limited funding, and this does mean that sometimes people don't get care as quickly as they should. The system can definitely be improved.

However, remember that this is based on spending only a little more than half what the US is spending on healthcare as a percent of GDP. If we were willing to spend an equivalent amount—15%—to what they are spending in the States, we could virtually eliminate waiting times and many other inherent imperfections in the current system.

National Health Service Belongs to the People

It is there to improve our health and well-being, supporting us to keep mentally and physically well, to get better when we are ill and, when we cannot fully recover, to stay as well as we can to the end of our lives. It works at the limits of science—bringing the highest levels of human knowledge and skill to save lives and improve health. It touches our lives at times of basic human need, when care and compassion are what matter most.

The NHS is founded on a common set of principles and values that bind together the communities and people it serve—patients and public—and the staff who work for it.

National Health Service,
NHS Constitution, *January 21, 2009.*
www.nhs.uk.

That is not to say that an NHS-style system is right for the USA—I don't think it is. But having lived under both systems I can tell you that if given the choice of living under the NHS or under the US insurance system, I would have no hesitation in choosing the NHS, even if only for career reasons. What do I mean by career reasons? Well, I recently parted company with my former employer and am working as an independent consultant. This career move would have been impossible for me in America—I would have had to either cling desperately to my previous employer at all costs, or to take a 9 to 5 job (any job) just to ensure I am covered. Living under universal health care has allowed me the freedom to pursue my own happiness. That's surely something that Americans everywhere support.

If you are an American living in Europe, now might be a good time to pick up the phone to your relatives back home and give them the real story about your experiences with health care overseas. I bet they'd love to hear from you.

> "[The American health care system] is not inferior to other developed countries' systems—and we should therefore not be looking to these systems, most of which are characterized by heavy government intervention, for inspiration."

The Universal Health Care Systems of Other Countries Provide Lower Quality Health Care

John C. Goodman

John C. Goodman, founder and president of the National Center for Policy Analysis, argues in the following viewpoint that while the American health care system has problems, it is not inferior to other countries'. In fact, patients in the United States are screened more frequently for diseases such as prostate cancer and breast cancer, and therefore have better access to preventive care. Goodman believes that if we look at the disease and not just the numbers, the United States has a higher success rate for cancer patients, hip replacements, and more.

As you read, consider the following questions:

1. According to the author, what is one reason why people may be inclined to hold back on preventive care?

2. According to the viewpoint, does the United States or Europe have a higher survival rate among cancer patients?

3. As stated in the viewpoint, what factors "make it increasingly easy to obtain insurance after becoming ill"?

The health-care systems of all developed countries face three unrelenting problems: rising costs, inadequate quality, and incomplete access to care. A slew of recent articles, published mainly in medical journals, suggest that the health-care systems of other countries are superior to ours on all these fronts. Yet the articles are at odds with a substantial economic literature.

What follows is a brief review of the evidence. As other writers demonstrate elsewhere in this issue, the American health-care system has plenty of problems. But it is not inferior to other developed countries' systems—and we should therefore not be looking to these systems, most of which are characterized by heavy government intervention, for inspiration.

The Misleading Statistics

Taken at face value, international statistics show that the United States spends more than twice as much per person on health care as the average developed country. But these statistics are misleading. Other countries are far more aggressive than we are at disguising and shifting costs—for example, by using the power of government purchase to artificially suppress the incomes of doctors, nurses, and hospital personnel. This makes their aggregate outlays look smaller when all that has really happened is that part of the cost has been shifted from one group (patients and taxpayers) to another (health-care providers). This is equivalent to taxing doctors, nurses, or some other group so that others may pay less for their care.

Normal market forces have been so suppressed throughout the developed world that the prices paid for medical services rarely reflect the services' actual cost. As a result, adding all these prices together produces aggregate numbers in which one can have little confidence. One gets a better measure of how much countries spend by looking at the real resources used; and by that measure, the U.S. system is pretty good. For example, we use fewer doctors than the average developed country to produce the same or better outcomes. We also use fewer nurses and fewer hospital beds, make fewer physician visits, and spend fewer days in the hospital. About the only thing we use more of is technology.

Spending totals aside, the U.S. has been neither worse nor better than the rest of the developed world at controlling spending growth. The average annual rate of growth of real per capita U.S. health-care spending is slightly below the OECD [Organisation for Economic Co-operation and Development] average over the past four decades (4.4 percent versus 4.5 percent). It appears that other developed countries are traveling down the same spending path we are.

Examining the Disease Instead of the Statistics

Critics point to the fact that U.S. life expectancy is in the middle of the pack among developed countries, and that our infant-mortality rate is among the highest. But are these the right measures? Within the U.S., life expectancy at birth varies greatly between racial and ethnic groups, from state to state, and across counties. These differences are thought to reflect such lifestyle choices as diet, exercise, and smoking. Infant mortality varies by a factor of two or three across racial and ethnic lines, and from city to city and state to state, for reasons apparently having little to do with health care.

All too often, the heterogeneous population of the United States is compared with the homogeneous populations of European countries. A state such as Utah compares favorably with almost any developed country. Texas, with its high minority population, tends to compare unfavorably. But these outcomes have almost nothing to do with the doctors and hospitals in the two states.

It makes far more sense to look at the diseases and conditions to which we know medical science can make a real difference—cancer, diabetes, and hypertension, for example. The largest international study to date found that the five-year survival rate for all types of cancer among both men and women was higher in the U.S. than in Europe. There is a steeper increase in blood pressure with advancing age in Europe, and a 60 percent higher prevalence of hypertension. The aggressive treatment offered to U.S. cardiac patients apparently improves survival and functioning relative to that of Canadian patients. Fewer health- and disability-related problems occur among U.S. spinal-cord-injury patients than among Canadian and British patients.

The United States Has Better Access to Treatment

Britain has only one-fourth as many CT scanners per capita as the U.S., and one-third as many MRI scanners. The rate at which the British provide coronary-bypass surgery or angioplasty to heart patients is only one-fourth the U.S. rate, and hip replacements are only two-thirds the U.S. rate. The rate for treating kidney failure (dialysis or transplant) is five times higher in the U.S. for patients between the ages of 45 and 84, and nine times higher for patients 85 years or older.

Overall, nearly 1.8 million Britons are waiting for hospital or outpatient treatments at any given time. In 2002–2004, di-

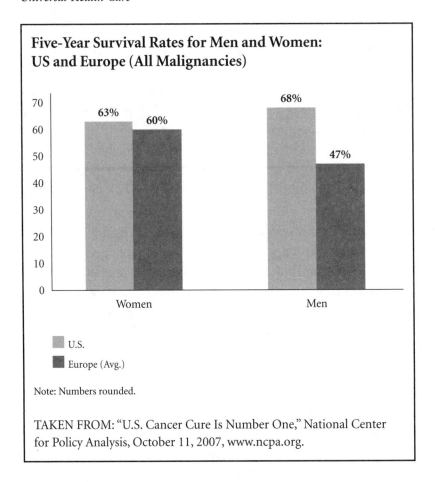

Five-Year Survival Rates for Men and Women: US and Europe (All Malignancies)

Note: Numbers rounded.

TAKEN FROM: "U.S. Cancer Cure Is Number One," National Center for Policy Analysis, October 11, 2007, www.ncpa.org.

alysis patients waited an average of 16 days for permanent blood-vessel access in the U.S., 20 days in Europe, and 62 days in Canada. In 2000, Norwegian patients waited an average of 133 days for hip replacement, 63 days for cataract surgery, 160 days for a knee replacement, and 46 days for bypass surgery after being approved for treatment. Short waits for cataract surgery produce better outcomes, prompt coronary-artery bypass reduces mortality, and rapid hip replacement reduces disability and death. Studies show that only 5 percent of Americans wait more than four months for surgery, compared with 23 percent of Australians, 26 percent of New Zealanders, 27 percent of Canadians, and 36 percent of Britons.

The United States Has Higher Amount of Preventive Care

If people have to pay for care directly, it is often claimed, they will be inclined to skimp on preventive care—care that can catch diseases in their early stages, saving lives and money. Yet the proportion of middle-aged Canadian women who have never had a mammogram is twice that of the U.S., and three times as many Canadian women have never had a Pap smear. Fewer than a fifth of Canadian men have ever been tested for prostate-specific antigen, compared with about half of American men. Only one in ten adult Canadians has had a colonoscopy, compared with about a third of adult Americans.

These differences in screening may partly explain why the mortality rate in Canada is 25 percent higher for breast cancer, 18 percent higher for prostate cancer, and 13 percent higher for colorectal cancer. In addition, while half of all diabetics have high blood pressure, it is controlled in 36 percent of U.S. cases, compared with only 9 percent of cases in Canada.

Transitory Uninsurance in the United States

Of the 46 million nominally uninsured, about 12 million are eligible for such public programs as Medicaid and the State Children's Health Insurance Program (S-CHIP). They can usually enroll even at the time of treatment, arguably making them de facto insured. About 17 million of the uninsured are living in households with annual incomes of at least $50,000. More than half of those earn more than $75,000, suggesting that they are uninsured by choice.

Like unemployment, uninsurance is usually transitory: 75 percent of uninsured spells last one year or less, and 91 percent last two years or less. Although the fraction of the population with health insurance rises and falls with the business cycle, it has been fairly constant for the past two decades, despite an unprecedented influx of immigrants with an uninsurance rate 2.5 times that of the native-born population. Guaranteed-issue laws, state high-risk pools, and retroactive Medicaid eligibility make it increasingly easy to obtain insurance after becoming ill.

Unequal Access to Health Care

Aneurin Bevan, father of the British National Health Service (NHS), declared, "The essence of a satisfactory health service is that rich and poor are treated alike, that poverty is not a disability and wealth is not advantaged." More than 30 years after the NHS's founding, an official task force found little evidence that it had equalized health-care access. Another study, 20 years later, concluded that access had become more unequal in the years between the two studies.

In Canada, the wealthy and powerful have significantly greater access to medical specialists than do the less well-connected poor. High-profile patients enjoy more frequent services, shorter waiting times, and greater choice of specialists. Moreover, non-elderly, white, low-income Canadians are 22 percent more likely to be in poor health than their U.S. counterparts.

In developed countries generally, among people with similar health conditions, high earners use the system more intensely, and use costlier services, than do low earners. It seems likely that the personal characteristics that ensure success in a market economy also enhance success in bureaucratic systems.

| *"The vast majority of Canadians get the vast majority of what they need the vast majority of the time."*

The Canadian Single-Payer System Provides a Good Model for Universal Coverage in the United States

Sara Robinson

In this viewpoint Sara Robinson, a fellow at the Campaign for America's Future and a consulting partner with Cognitive Policy Works in Seattle, addresses ten myths about the Canadian health care system, a single-payer system that is a frequent target of opponents of universal health care. Robinson argues that the Canadian health care model, while not perfect, does provide a useful example of one way that universal health care can be implemented.

As you read, consider the following questions:

1. The author says she is "both a health-card-carrying Canadian resident and an uninsured American citizen. . . ."

Sara Robinson, "Mythbusting Canadian Healthcare—Part I," *Campaign for America's Future*, February 4, 2008. Reproduced by permission.

Does this put her in a unique position to discuss the pros and cons of the U.S. and Canadian health care systems? Why or why not?

2. What are some of the ways the Canadian single-payer system benefits doctors, according to the author of this viewpoint?

3. The author provides a list of "basics," costs that are covered by the Canadian health care system. What items are included on this list?

2008 is shaping up to be the election year that we finally get to have the Great American Healthcare Debate again. Harry and Louise are back with a vengeance. [Harry and Louise were characters in anti–health care reform ads that ran in the 1990s.] Conservatives are rumbling around the talk show circuit bellowing about the socialist threat to the (literal) American body politic. And, as usual, Canada is once again getting dragged into the fracas, shoved around by both sides as either an exemplar or a warning—and, along the way, getting coated with the obfuscating dust of so many willful misconceptions that the actual facts about How Canada Does It are completely lost in the melee.

I'm both a health-care-card-carrying Canadian resident and an uninsured American citizen who regularly sees doctors on both sides of the border. As such, I'm in a unique position to address the pros and cons of both systems first-hand. If we're going to have this conversation, it would be great if we could start out (for once) with actual facts, instead of ideological posturing, wishful thinking, hearsay, and random guessing about how things get done up here.

To that end, this article aims at busting the common myths Americans routinely tell each other about Canadian health care. When the right-wing hysterics drag out these hoary old bogeymen, this time, we need to be armed and ready to blast them into straw. Because, mostly, straw is all they're made of.

1. *Canada's health care system is "socialized medicine."*

False. In socialized medical systems, the doctors work directly for the state. In Canada (and many other countries with universal care), doctors run their own private practices, just like they do in the U.S. The only difference is that every doctor deals with one insurer, instead of 150. And that insurer is the provincial government, which is accountable to the legislature and the voters if the quality of coverage is allowed to slide.

The proper term for this is "single-payer insurance." In talking to Americans about it, the better phrase is "Medicare for all."

2. *Doctors are hurt financially by single-payer health care.*

True and *False.* Doctors in Canada do make less than their US counterparts. But they also have lower overhead, and usually much better working conditions. A few reasons for this:

First, as noted, they don't have to charge higher fees to cover the salary of a full-time staffer to deal with over a hundred different insurers, all of whom are bent on denying care whenever possible. In fact, most Canadian doctors get by quite nicely with just one assistant, who cheerfully handles the phones, mail, scheduling, patient reception, stocking, filing, and billing all by herself in the course of a standard workday.

Second, they don't have to spend several hours every day on the phone cajoling insurance company bean counters into doing the right thing by their patients. My doctor in California worked a 70-hour week: 35 hours seeing patients, and another 35 hours on the phone arguing with insurance companies. My Canadian doctor, on the other hand, works a 35-hour week, period. She files her invoices online, and the vast majority are simply paid—quietly, quickly, and without hassle. There is no runaround. There are no fights. Appointments aren't interrupted by vexing phone calls. Care is seldom denied (because everybody knows the rules). She gets her checks on time, sees her patients on schedule, takes Thursdays off, and gets home in time for dinner.

One unsurprising side effect of all this is that the doctors I see here are, to a person, more focused, more relaxed, more generous with their time, more up-to-date in their specialties, and overall much less distracted from the real work of doctoring. You don't realize how much stress ... American doctor-insurer fights put on the day-to-day quality of care until you see doctors who don't operate under that stress, because they never have to fight those battles at all. Amazingly: they seem to enjoy their jobs.

Third: The average American medical student graduates $140,000 in hock. The average Canadian doctor's debt is roughly half that.

Finally, Canadian doctors pay lower malpractice insurance fees. When paying for health care constitutes one of a family's major expenses, expectations tend to run very high. A doctor's mistake not only damages the body; it may very well throw a middle-class family permanently into the ranks of the working poor, and render the victim uninsurable for life. With so much at stake, it's no wonder people are quick to rush to court for redress.

Canadians are far less likely to sue in the first place, since they're not having to absorb devastating financial losses in addition to any physical losses when something goes awry. The cost of the damaging treatment will be covered. So will the cost of fixing it. And, no matter what happens, the victim will remain insured for life. When lawsuits do occur, the awards don't have to include coverage for future medical costs, which reduces the insurance company's liability.

3. *Wait times in Canada are horrendous.*

True and *False* again—it depends on which province you live in, and what's wrong with you. Canada's health care system runs on federal guidelines that ensure uniform standards of care, but each territory and province administers its own program. Some provinces don't plan their facilities well enough; in those, you can have waits. Some do better. As a general rule, the farther north you live, the harder it is to get to care, simply because the doctors and hospitals are concentrated in the south. But that's just as true in any rural county in the U.S.

You can hear the bitching about it no matter where you live, though. The percentage of Canadians who'd consider giving up their beloved system consistently languishes in the single digits. A few years ago, a TV show asked Canadians to name the Greatest Canadian in history; and in a broad national consensus, they gave the honor to Tommy Douglas, the Saskatchewan premier who is considered the father of the country's health care system. . . . In spite of that, though, grousing about health care is still unofficially Canada's third national sport after curling and hockey.

And for the country's newspapers, it's a prime watchdogging opportunity. Any little thing goes sideways at the local hospital, and it's on the front pages the next day. Those kinds of stories sell papers, because everyone is invested in that system and has a personal stake in how well it functions. The American system might benefit from this kind of constant scrutiny, because it's certainly one of the things that keeps the quality high. But it also makes people think it's far worse than it is.

Critics should be reminded that the American system is not exactly instant-on, either. When I lived in California, I had excellent insurance, and got my care through one of the best university-based systems in the nation. Yet I routinely had to wait anywhere from six to twelve weeks to get in to see a specialist. Non-emergency surgical waits could be anywhere from four weeks to four months. After two years in the BC [British Columbia] system, I'm finding the experience to be pretty much comparable, and often better. The notable exception is MRIs [magnetic resonance imaging], which were easy in California, but can take many months to get here. (It's the number one thing people go over the border for.) Other than that, urban Canadians get care about as fast as urban Americans do.

4. *You have to wait forever to get a family doctor.*

False for the vast majority of Canadians, but *True* for a few. Again, it all depends on where you live. I live in suburban Vancouver, and there are any number of first-rate GPs in my neighborhood who are taking new patients. If you don't have a working relationship with one, but need to see a doctor now, there are 24-hour urgent care clinics in most neighborhoods that will usually get you in and out on the minor stuff in under an hour.

It is, absolutely, harder to get to a doctor if you live out in a small town, or up in the territories. But that's just as true in the U.S.—and in America, the government won't cover the airfare for rural folk to come down to the city for needed treatment, which all the provincial plans do.

5. *You don't get to choose your own doctor.*

Scurrilously [characterized by abuse and slander] False. Somebody, somewhere, is getting paid a lot of money to make this kind of stuff up. The cons love to scare the kids with stones about the government picking your doctor for you, and you don't get a choice. Be afraid! Be very afraid!

For the record: Canadians pick their own doctors, just like Americans do. And not only that: since it all pays the same, poor Canadians have exactly the same access to the country's top specialists that rich ones do.

6. *Canada's care plan only covers the basics. You're still on your own for any extras, including prescription drugs. And you still have to pay for it.*

True—but not as big an issue as you might think. The province does charge a small monthly premium (ours is $108/ month for a family of four) for the basic coverage. However, most people never even have to write that check: almost all

For Fewer Dollars, Better Care

By many measures, Canadians are healthier than Americans, with a longer lifespan and lower infant mortality, even though they spend much less on medical care. Canadians devote about 10 percent of their gross domestic product, the total of a nation's goods and services, to provide full health coverage for all citizens. American health costs account for about 14 percent of GDP, yet 45 million Americans have no health insurance and many more have limited coverage.

One of the main culprits pushing up the cost of care in the United States is the expense of administering a plethora of complicated health plans. It has been estimated that any large health insurer in a midsize U.S. state spends more on administration than is spent on health administration in all Canada.

Barry Brown,
"In Critical Condition: Health Care in America Canada's Way,"
SF Gate, October 14, 2004.
http://www.sfgate.com/cgi-bin/article.cgi?f=/
c/a/2004/10/14/BUGR28JFEN59.DTL.

employers pick up the tab for their employees' premiums as part of the standard benefits package; and the province covers it for people on public assistance or disability.

"The basics" covered by this plan include 100% of all doctor's fees, ambulance fares, tests, and everything that happens in a hospital—in other words, the really big-ticket items that routinely drive American families into bankruptcy. In BC, it doesn't include "extras" like medical equipment, prescriptions, physical therapy or chiropractic care, dental, vision, and so on; and if you want a private or semi-private room with

TV and phone, that costs extra (about what you'd pay for a room in a middling hotel). That other stuff does add up; but it's far easier to afford if you're not having to cover the big expenses, too. Furthermore: you can deduct [off your income taxes] any out-of-pocket health expenses you do have to pay. . . . And, as every American knows by now, drugs aren't nearly as expensive here, either.

Filling the gap between the basics and the extras is the job of the country's remaining private health insurers. Since they're off the hook for the ruinously expensive big-ticket items that can put their own profits at risk, the insurance companies make a tidy business out of offering inexpensive policies that cover all those smaller, more predictable expenses. Top-quality add-on policies typically run in the ballpark of $75 per person in a family per month—about $300 for a family of four—if you're stuck buying an individual plan. Group plans are cheap enough that even small employers can afford to offer them as a routine benefit. An average working Canadian with employer-paid basic care and supplemental insurance gets free coverage equal to the best policies now only offered at a few of America's largest corporations. And that employer is probably only paying a couple hundred dollars a month to provide that benefit.

7. Canadian drugs are not the same.

More preposterous bogosity [false]. They are exactly the same drugs, made by the same pharmaceutical companies, often in the same factories. The Canadian drug distribution system, however, has much tighter oversight; and pharmacies and pharmacists are more closely regulated. If there is a difference in Canadian drugs at all, they're actually likely to be safer.

Also: pharmacists here dispense what the doctors tell them to dispense, the first time, without moralizing. I know. It's amazing.

8. Publicly-funded programs will inevitably lead to rationed health care, particularly for the elderly.

False. And bogglingly so. The papers would have a field day if there was the barest hint that this might be true.

One of the things that constantly amazes me here is how well cared for the elderly and disabled you see on the streets here are. No, these people are not being thrown out on the curb. In fact, they live longer, healthier, and more productive lives because they're getting a constant level of care that ensures small things get treated before they become big problems.

The health care system also makes it easier on their caregiving adult children, who have more time to look in on Mom and take her on outings because they aren't working 60-hour weeks trying to hold onto a job that gives them insurance.

9. People won't be responsible for their own health if they're not being forced to pay for the consequences.

False. The philosophical basis of America's privatized health care system might best be characterized as medical Calvinism. It's fascinating to watch well-educated secularists who recoil at the Protestant obsession with personal virtue, prosperity as a cardinal sign of election by God, and total responsibility for one's own salvation turn into fire-eyed, moralizing True Believers when it comes to the subject of Taking Responsibility For One's Own Health.

They'll insist that health, like salvation, is entirely in our own hands. If you just have the character and self-discipline to stick to an abstemious regime of careful diet, clean living, and frequent sweat offerings to the Great Treadmill God, you'll never get sick. (Like all good theologies, there's even an unspoken promise of immortality: if you do it really really right, they imply, you might even live forever.) The virtuous Elect can be discerned by their svelte figures and low cholesterol numbers. From here, it's a short leap to the conviction that those who suffer from chronic conditions are victims of their own weaknesses and simply getting what they deserve.

Part of their punishment is being forced to pay for the expensive, heavily marketed pharmaceuticals needed to alleviate these avoidable illnesses. They can't complain. It was their own damned fault; and it's not our responsibility to pay for their sins. In fact, it's recently been suggested that they be shunned, lest they lead the virtuous into sin.

Of course, this is bad theology whether you're applying it to the state of one's soul or one's arteries. The fact is that bad genes, bad luck, and the ravages of age eventually take their toll on all of us—even the most careful of us. The economics of the Canadian system reflect this very different philosophy: it's built on the belief that maintaining health is not an individual responsibility, but a collective one. Since none of us controls fate, the least we can do is be there for each other as our numbers come up.

This difference is expressed in a few different ways. First: Canadians tend to think of tending to one's health as one of your duties as a citizen. You do what's right because you don't want to take up space in the system, or put that burden on your fellow taxpayers. Second, "taking care of yourself" has a slightly expanded definition here, which includes a greater emphasis on public health. Canadians are serious about not coming to work if you're contagious, and seeing a doctor ASAP [as soon as possible] if you need to. Staying healthy includes not only diet and exercise; but also taking care to keep your germs to yourself, avoiding stress, and getting things treated while they're still small and cheap to fix.

Third, there's a somewhat larger awareness that stress leads to big-ticket illnesses—and a somewhat lower cultural tolerance for employers who put people in high-stress situations. Nobody wants to pick up the tab for their greed. And finally, there's a generally greater acceptance on the part of both the elderly and their families that end-of-life heroics may be drawing resources away from people who might put them to better use. You can have them if you want them; but reasonable and compassionate people should be able to take the larger view.

The bottom line: When it comes to getting people to make healthy choices, appealing to their sense of the common good seems to work at least as well as Calvinist moralizing.

10. *This all sounds great—but the taxes to cover it are just unaffordable. And besides, isn't the system in bad financial shape?*

False. On one hand, our annual Canadian tax bite runs about 10% higher than our U.S. taxes did. On the other, we're not paying out the equivalent of two new car payments every month to keep the family insured here. When you balance out the difference, we're actually money ahead. When you factor in the greatly increased social stability that follows when everybody's getting their necessary health care, the impact on our quality of life becomes even more significant.

And True—but only because this is a universal truth that we need to make our peace with. Yes, the provincial plans are always struggling. So is every single publicly-funded health care system in the world, including the VA [the U.S. Department of Veteran Affairs] and Medicare. There's always tension between what the users of the system want and what the taxpayers are willing to pay. The balance of power ebbs and flows between them; but no matter where it lies at any given moment, at least one of the pair is always going to be at least somewhat unhappy.

But, as many of us know all too well, there's also constant tension between what patients want and what private insurers are willing to pay. At least when it's in government hands, we can demand some accountability. And my experience in Canada has convinced me that this accountability is what makes all the difference between the two systems.

It is true that Canada's system is not the same as the U.S. system. It's designed to deliver a somewhat different product, to a population that has somewhat different expectations. But the end result is that the vast majority of Canadians get the vast majority of what they need the vast majority of the time. It'll be a good day when Americans can hold their heads high and proudly make that same declaration.

> "We definitely need universal coverage in the United States. But we do not need to go to a single-payer system to achieve that goal."

The Canadian Model for Achieving Universal Health Care Is Not a Good One for the United States

George C. Halvorson

In this viewpoint George C. Halvorson, chairman and chief executive officer of Kaiser Foundation Health Plan, Inc., and Kaiser Foundation Hospitals, argues that a single-payer health care model, like that employed by Canada, is not the right way for the United States to achieve universal health care coverage. In Canada, savings are achieved through strict cost controls that affect the incomes of physicians and nurses. In addition, the government controls hospital budgets, resulting in lower levels of investment in medical equipment and technology.

George C. Halvorson, "Understanding the Trade-offs of the Canadian Health System," *Healthcare Financial Management*, October 2007, pp. 82–84. Copyright © 2007 Healthcare Financial Management Association. All rights reserved. Reproduced by permission.

As you read, consider the following questions:

1. How much do physician office visits cost in the United States and in Nova Scotia? According to the author of the viewpoint, what accounts for the difference?

2. How does the Canadian government manage the costs of prescription drugs?

3. What is the annual per-person cost of health care in Canada? In the United States? How does the author explain the significance of this difference?

Americans are increasingly asking why the United States is the only western industrialized country that has not managed to achieve universal healthcare coverage for all of its citizens. They also are wondering why we don't learn from our neighbors to the north and move the current Canadian universal coverage approach south. That's an interesting and important question.

Canada provides universal coverage to all of its citizens while spending less money on health care than the United States does by a significant margin. The question we need to ask ourselves as data-oriented healthcare financial people is, how does the Canadian system achieve these goals? The answer might surprise you.

Most people who know that Canada spends less money on health care believe that the cost difference is almost entirely due to the lower administrative costs that result from Canada using a "single-payer" insurance model. Is that true? No.

The truth is that Canada now spends about $2,600 per resident per year less than we spend on healthcare costs in the United States because—very simply—Canadians spend less money on the actual purchase of care.

How do they do that? First, by setting fees. Fees are much lower in Canada. A physician office visit that costs $80 to $100 in the United States costs only $28.60 in Nova Scotia.

The government of each Canadian province determines the exact fee schedule and price list for every physician in the province—and those Canadian fee schedules for physicians are set far below U.S. fee schedules.

Canada's Pricing Model

Those of us who work in healthcare finance in this country should be at least slightly familiar with the Canadian pricing model, because in those cases where our government is now the actual direct payer for care, we already use a very similar approach. Our government pays roughly $60 for an office visit for each Medicare patient and pays well under $50 per visit if the patient is on Medicaid.

So physicians in Canada make less money on each patient than physicians in the United States do, and the total impact of those payment differences makes up a major portion of the difference in care costs between the two countries.

For hospital care, the Canadian government doesn't set fees to control costs; instead, it directly controls each hospital's budget. The government of each province sets a specific annual budget for each local hospital, and the government expects each hospital in the province to operate within its assigned budget. Canadian provinces don't like to raise taxes to increase hospital budgets, so the local budgets are far lower than U.S. hospital revenue streams. Those hospital payment levels are likely to stay far lower until Canadian voters offer to pay more in taxes. "No new taxes" has the same political charm in Canada that it has in the United States, so the people who run Canadian hospitals are not expecting big budget increases soon.

Tight individual budgets mean that Canadian hospitals can't invest in medical equipment or new technology as easily as U.S. hospitals can. You can see the results in many spending areas.

The Trouble with Canadian Health Care

• The Canadian single-payer system does not cover prescription drugs on a universal basis. Only about one-third of the Canadian population is eligible for various government-financed drug programs. The remainder of the population has private-sector drug insurance coverage or pays cash for outpatient drugs, just like in the United States.

• Public drug plans in Canada often refuse to cover new drugs. On average, only 44 percent of all new drugs that were approved as safe and effective by the Canadian government in 2004 were actually covered by government drug insurance programs in October 2007.

Brett J. Skinner,
"The Trouble with Canadian Healthcare,"
The American, *December 6, 2008.*
www.american.com.

Relatively long waiting times for some kinds of surgery in Canada tend to be a direct and logical consequence of tight local hospital budgets. When money is tight or runs out, care slows. One of the beauties and virtues of the Canadian system is the absolute equality of access for all citizens. So when care slows for anyone in an area, it slows for everyone in that area—unless you are a well-to-do Canadian who can afford to cross the border to buy your care more quickly in the United States. Canada does not pay for that "external" care.

It would obviously be a challenging process to convert all U.S. hospitals to the Canadian fixed-budget model.

Prescription Drug Coverage

So how do Canadian provinces deal with drug costs? Again, very simply. Seven of eight provinces do not cover prescription drugs at all. People in those provinces buy their own "non-hospital" drugs. Every province carefully negotiates the price of all drugs with the drug companies, and then most people in Canada reach into their own pockets to buy their medications.

That direct-payment approach is not likely to be welcomed by the roughly 250 million U.S. citizens who have some form of prescription drug coverage, but it probably would reduce drug costs in the United States if we used it here.

Canada does allow its citizens to but separate drug coverage from private insurers. Many do.

Administrative Costs

I mentioned earlier that most people believe, inaccurately, that the primary area where Canada saves the most money is in administrative costs. What are the real numbers there? Health-care administrative costs in the United States run between 10 percent and 15 percent of total healthcare costs. Canadian administrative costs run closer to 5 percent. (The Commonwealth Fund estimates total U.S. administrative costs at roughly 8 percent, while the Government Accountability Office estimate of U.S. administrative costs comes closer to 12 percent.) Estimates of current American and Canadian cost levels differ a bit from source to source. But we know enough to answer a very basic question: Using relatively conservative estimates, how much of the total cost difference between the two countries actually comes from the administrative cost factor?

Do the math. It's relatively easy to calculate. If total health-care costs per person are about $5,600 in the United States and about $3,000 in Canada, the total per-person care cost difference is $2,600.

How much of that difference is due to administrative costs? Let's assume that the actual administrative cost difference between the two countries is a full 10 percent (5 percent costs for Canada, 15 percent costs for the United States). Ten percent of the total $5,600 U.S. cost is $560. In other words, U.S. administrative costs would be $560 lower per person if the Canadian administrative cost levels were achieved here. Cutting that entire 10 percent completely out of total U.S. health-care costs would still leave a pure care-based cost difference of slightly over $2,000 per person per year. In other words, the vast majority of the actual cost difference between the two countries is not due to administrative cost differences. Lower total costs in Canada result overwhelmingly from major differences in the actual cost of care, not administration.

The single-payer approach to healthcare cost controls creates a very different economic reality for Canadian and U.S. caregivers. Tenured registered nurses in California and New York make more money than primary care physicians in Canada—up to 25 percent more money for a 10-year nurse in California compared with a hospital-based primary care physician north of the border. The Canadian single-payer system has a very high level of control over caregiver pay levels and paychecks. As a result, in Canada, caregivers make significantly less money.

Achieving Universal Coverage

We definitely need universal coverage in the United States. But we do not need to go to a single-payer system to achieve that goal. Most European countries have achieved universal coverage by using a combination of private health plans, government programs, individual consumer mandates, subsidized or free coverage for low-income people, and a private market-place for hospitals, physicians, and other caregivers. We Americans need to figure out what combination of those factors would best meet the needs of our citizens and let us achieve universal coverage here.

Some aspects of the Canadian approach—the ones that actually save all the money (tight medical fees, absolute and rigid hospital budgets, lower caregiver income levels, no drug coverage, and having all medical claims paid by the provinces rather than by private insurers)—might be a bit more difficult to implement here than a more typical European model of universal coverage that offers more choices, adequate drug coverage, shorter waiting times for care, and fewer direct provider controls. We have some choices to make. Let's make them wisely, knowing what options we actually have.

> "The lower income of French physicians is allayed by two factors. Practice liability is greatly diminished by a tort-averse legal system, and medical schools, although extremely competitive to enter, are tuition-free."

The French Model for Universal Health Care Is Better than the Canadian Model

Paul V. Dutton

In this viewpoint Paul V. Dutton, an associate professor of history at Northern Arizona University, argues that the French health care system, which was rated as best in the world by the World Health Organization in 2001, is the best model for the United States to follow as it moves toward universal health care coverage.

As you read, consider the following questions:

1. What are two similarities between the U.S. and the French health care systems that are highlighted by the author?

Paul V. Dutton, "France's Model Healthcare System," *The Boston Globe*, August 11, 2007.

2. Although French physicians earn significantly less than physicians in the United States, the author suggests that they enjoy other financial advantages. What are they?

3. Why, according to the author, are the French moving away from the requirement that health insurance expenses be paid by payroll and wage deductions? What source of funding will replace payroll and wage deductions?

Many advocates of a universal healthcare system in the United States look to Canada for their model. While the Canadian healthcare system has much to recommend it, there's another model that has been too long neglected. That is the healthcare system in France.

Although the French system faces many challenges, the World Health Organization rated it the best in the world in 2001 because of its universal coverage, responsive healthcare providers, patient and provider freedoms, and the health and longevity of the country's population. The United States ranked 37.

The French system is also not inexpensive. At $3,500 per capita it is one of the most costly in Europe, yet that is still far less than the $6,100 per person in the United States.

A System That Values Choice

An understanding of how France came to its healthcare system would be instructive in any renewed debate in the United States.

That's because the French share Americans' distaste for restrictions on patient choice and they insist on autonomous private practitioners rather than a British-style national health service, which the French dismiss as "socialized medicine." Virtually all physicians in France participate in the nation's public health insurance, Sécurité Sociale.

Their freedoms of diagnosis and therapy are protected in ways that would make their managed-care-controlled US counterparts envious. However, the average American physician earns more than five times the average US wage while the average French physician makes only about two times the average earnings of his or her compatriots. But the lower income of French physicians is allayed by two factors. Practice liability is greatly diminished by a tort-averse legal system, and medical schools, although extremely competitive to enter, are tuition-free. Thus, French physicians enter their careers with little if any debt and pay much lower malpractice insurance premiums.

Nor do France's doctors face the high nonmedical personnel payroll expenses that burden American physicians. Sécurité Sociale has created a standardized and speedy system for physician billing and patient reimbursement using electronic funds.

It's not uncommon to visit a French medical office and see no nonmedical personnel. What a concept. No back office army of billing specialists who do daily battle with insurers' arcane and constantly changing rules of payment.

Moreover, in contrast to Canada and Britain, there are no waiting lists for elective procedures and patients need not seek pre-authorizations. In other words, like in the United States, "rationing" is not a word that leaves the lips of hopeful politicians. How might the French case inform the US debate over healthcare reform?

National health insurance in France stands upon two grand historical bargains—the first with doctors and a second with insurers.

Doctors . . . agreed to participate in compulsory health insurance [only] if the law protected a patient's choice of practitioner and guaranteed physicians' control over medical decision-making. Given their current frustrations, America's doctors might finally be convinced to throw their support be-

The French Lesson in Health Care

To grasp how the French system works, think about Medicare for the elderly in the U.S., then expand that to encompass the entire population. French medicine is based on a widely held value that the healthy should pay for care of the sick. Everyone has access to the same basic coverage through national insurance funds, to which every employer and employee contributes. The government picks up the tab for the unemployed who cannot gain coverage through a family member.

"The French Lesson in Healthcare,"
BusinessWeek, *July 9, 2007.*

hind universal health insurance if it protected their professional judgment and created a sane system of billing and reimbursement.

A System That Is Privately Administered

French legislators also overcame insurance industry resistance by permitting the nation's already existing insurers to administer its new healthcare funds. Private health insurers are also central to the system as supplemental insurers who cover patient expenses that are not paid for by Sécurité Sociale. Indeed, nearly 90 percent of the French population possesses such coverage, making France home to a booming private health insurance market.

The French system strongly discourages the kind of experience rating that occurs in the United States, making it more difficult for insurers to deny coverage for pre-existing conditions or to those who are not in good health. In fact, in France, the sicker you are, the more coverage, care, and treatment you get. Would American insurance companies cut a comparable deal?

Like all healthcare systems, the French confront ongoing problems. Today French reformers' number one priority is to move health insurance financing away from payroll and wage levies because they hamper employers' willingness to hire. Instead, France is turning toward broad taxes on earned and unearned income alike to pay for healthcare.

American advocates of mandates on employers to provide health insurance should take note. The link between employment and health security is a historical artifact whose disadvantages now far outweigh its advantages. Economists estimate that between 25 and 45 percent of the US labor force is now job-locked. That is, employees make career decisions based on their need to maintain affordable health coverage or avoid exclusion based on a preexisting condition.

Perhaps it's time for us to take a closer look at French ideas about healthcare reform. They could become an import far less "foreign" and "unfriendly" than many here might initially imagine.

Periodical Bibliography

The following articles have been selected to supplement the diverse views presented in this chapter.

Kerry Capell   "Is Europe's Health Care Better?" *Business Week*, June 13, 2009.

Kerry Capell   "The French Lesson in Health Care," *Business Week*, July 9, 2007.

Holly Dressel   "Has Canada Got the Cure?" *Yes! Magazine*, Fall 2006.

Lafayette Academic News "Students Compare British and American Health-Care Systems," November 8, 2005.

Jim Landers   "Is the French Health System a Model for the U.S.?" *Dallas Morning News*, May 18, 2009.

Sarah Lyall   "Paying Patients Test British Health Care System," *New York Times*, February 21, 2008.

Neil Macdonald   "My Dear American Neighbours," *CBC News*, May 18, 2009.

Peter Morici   "Fixing American Health Care," *Finfacts Ireland*, May 19, 2009.

Jason Shafrin   "Health Care Around the Word," *Healthcare Economist*, April 14, 2008.

Robert Steinbrook   "Public Health Care in Canada," *New England Journal of Medicine*, April 20, 2006.

Michael Tanner   "The Grass Is Not Always Greener: A Look at National Health Care Systems Around the World," *Cato Institute*, March 2008.

Glenn Woiceshyn   "Canada's Healthcare System Is Bad Medicine," *Capitalism Magazine*, March 31, 2006.

OPPOSING VIEWPOINTS® SERIES

CHAPTER 4

What Steps Can the U.S. Take to Achieve Universal Health Care?

Chapter Preface

"The only risk is in doing nothing," Brian Higgins told a reporter for an upstate New York newspaper in the summer of 2009. "People's [health insurance] premiums will more than double over the next 10 years unless something is done . . . If nothing changes, millions in this country will be without health insurance because neither they nor their employers will be able to afford it."[1]

Higgins, a member of the House of Representatives from upstate New York, serves on the House Ways and Means Committee, one of several committees in the House and Senate that were working on a bill to reform the health care industry. Along with New York senators Chuck Schumer and Kirsten Gillibrand, Higgins was supporting the creation of a not-for-profit government-administered health insurance plan as an option for everyone. The so-called "public option" would be offered alongside an array of private insurance plans that are currently available, and individuals would be able to choose the plan that is right for them.

According to Schumer, several factors are driving support for a public option in New York, including lack of competition among private insurers, the rapidly escalating cost of health insurance, and an increase in the number of families who do not have access to any insurance at all. Schumer sees competition as key to addressing the problem, and believes that the introduction of a public option can satisfy that requirement. "The lack of competition is what drives up premiums," he said. . . . "Our current system, dominated by private insurance companies, simply has not done the job."

Schumer's diagnosis of the problem is agreed to be accurate by most parties in the health care debate. Yet the idea of a publicly funded alternative as the solution, even when offered alongside existing private insurance plans, has evoked intense opposition by some.

Particularly noteworthy is a statement to the Senate Finance Committee—one of the legislative bodies considering health care reform—by the American Medical Association. "The AMA does not believe that creating a public health insurance option for non-disabled individuals under age 65 is the best way to expand health insurance coverage and lower cost. The introduction of a new public plan threatens to restrict patient choice by driving out private insurers, which currently provide coverage for nearly 70 percent of Americans."[2] The AMA, which represents 250,000 physicians, does support the goal of affordable and universally accessible health insurance, and believes that insurance companies should not be allowed to deny coverage for pre-existing conditions, a key issue in health care reform. However, the organization believes this can best be accomplished through increased regulation of private insurance markets.

Not all physicians believe that the private insurance industry, even regulated, can provide the breadth and quality of care that is needed. Physicians for a National Health Program is an organization of medical doctors who actively support single-payer public health insurance—to the exclusion of private health insurance altogether. PNHP blames a "patchwork system of for-profit payers" for out-of-control health care costs in the United States, and believes that both physicians and patients would be better off with a single publicly funded health insurance plan. "Private insurers necessarily waste health dollars on things that have nothing to do with care: overhead, underwriting, billing, sales and marketing departments as well as huge profits and exorbitant executive pay," the PNHP Web site states. "Doctors and hospitals must maintain costly administrative staffs to deal with the bureaucracy. Combined, this needless administration consumes one-third (31 percent) of Americans' health dollars."

The debate over the desirability and possible scope of a publicly funded health insurance program is one facet of the ongoing conversation about health care reform. What other choices are available to policy-makers as they seek to reduce costs, increase competition, and make health care universally available? How can they best be implemented? Can existing programs provide a model for reform? What dangers and what advantages would various health care reforms present to patients, to providers, and to the private insurance industry? These are some of the questions that are considered in this chapter.

Notes

1. Kristen Johnson, "Status Quo Not an Option," *Jamestown Post-Journal*, August 2, 2009.
2. Robert Pear, "Doctors' Group Opposed Public Insurance Plan," *New York Times*, June 11, 2009.

> *"Multiple independent studies confirm that the administrative simplicity of a single universal insurance pool, like Medicare, yields savings that would allow comprehensive coverage for all at current levels of spending."*

Expansion of Medicare Is the Best Way to Provide Universal Access to Quality Health Care

Johnathon S. Ross

Johnathon S. Ross is a physician and the past president of Physicians for a National Health Program. In this viewpoint he argues that a single-payer universal insurance pool similar to Medicare, financed by payroll and individual taxes, is the simplest and most efficient way to be sure that health care is available to everyone who needs it.

As you read, consider the following questions:

1. According to the author, how many Americans die each year because they do not have health insurance?

Johnathon S. Ross, "A Genuine Cure for Our Health Care Woes," *Toledo Blade*, December 20, 2008. Reproduced by permission.

2. Why does the author criticize the Massachusetts approach to universal health care?

3. What does the author mean by "Medicare for all"?

With new leadership in place, America can end a national disgrace. Forty-six million of our friends, family and neighbors have no health care coverage at all. The Institute of Medicine estimates that over 18,000 Americans die each year from lack of health insurance alone. Tens of millions more risk bankruptcy because they have bare-bones insurance. Our troubled economy will only worsen this sad situation.

Senate Democrats are poised to prescribe a health reform proposal that will likely be based on a national insurance exchange, similar to the Federal Employees Health Benefit Program. The plan will probably mirror the reform proposals that President-elect Barack Obama made during his [2008] campaign.

Under this plan, federal oversight would increase regulation of the insurance plans that participate. The insurance exchange would guarantee coverage to all who purchase coverage, even those with pre-existing health conditions. Low-income individuals and families who do not qualify for the State Children's Health Insurance Program (SCHIP) or Medicaid would receive subsidies toward the purchase of insurance through the exchange.

Large businesses that do not offer insurance to their employees would be required to contribute a percentage of their payroll to the exchange to help their employees purchase coverage. Small businesses may receive tax credits to help them purchase insurance for their employees. The program will likely include a mandate that requires everyone, or nearly everyone, to have health insurance or pay a fine.

Does this plan sound complicated? It is. It requires regulating hundreds of insurers who consistently strive to avoid sick (and therefore more expensive) patients. It requires regulating thousands of businesses to confirm they cover their employees or pay into the exchange, and it requires finding and fining those who do not buy insurance. The complexity of handling millions of subsidized individual health insurance policies purchased through the new exchange will cost an estimated $100 billion yearly. Yet many people will likely remain uninsured.

The Massachusetts Model

Massachusetts is held out as the latest model. Half of the uninsured remain without coverage despite substantial expansions of Medicaid and subsidies for the purchase of private insurance. Massachusetts has yet to confront the issue of fining those who fail to purchase insurance. Costs continue to rise sharply. This is no surprise because this approach keeps the private, for-profit insurers at its center.

Similar to our current setup, each insurer, hospital, and doctor must keep track of myriad contracts, discount arrangements, benefit packages, formularies, limited referral networks, and insurance rules designed to reduce utilization and to increase the insurers' profits. This paperwork, which has nothing to do with delivering care, is a huge waste of resources.

Currently, insurers keep 15–20 percent of the premium dollar for their operating costs and for shareholder profits. Why would they want to reduce spending if they get to keep nearly one-fifth of whatever we spend?

Massachusetts is not alone in finding universal coverage and cost control impossible using this model of reform. Such was the experience in at least seven states where such a model has been tried before. Do we really want to multiply this complex state experiment by 50 before we see if it can actually work?

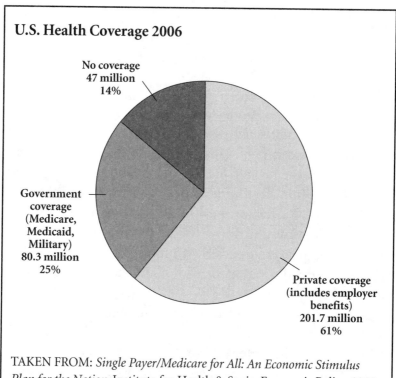

U.S. Health Coverage 2006

No coverage
47 million
14%

Government
coverage
(Medicare,
Medicaid,
Military)
80.3 million
25%

Private coverage
(includes employer
benefits)
201.7 million
61%

TAKEN FROM: *Single Payer/Medicare for All: An Economic Stimulus Plan for the Nation*, Institute for Health & Socio-Economic Policy, 2008. www.calnurses.org.

A Better Way

There is an alternative, however—a proven cure for our health care woes. Physicians for a National Health Program, a membership organization of tens of thousands of physicians from across the county, prescribes a nonprofit, single-payer national health insurance program as outlined in H.R. 676, the U.S. National Health Insurance Act.

This legislation establishes an improved and expanded Medicare for all. Everyone is automatically enrolled. Payroll and individual taxes replace private insurance premiums and out-of-pocket payments. This creates a single insurance pool adequate to cover all with no additional spending.

How can this be? Multiple independent studies confirm that the administrative simplicity of a single universal insurance pool, like Medicare, yields savings that would allow comprehensive coverage for all at current levels of spending. A tax-based public system is simple and efficient. Medicare spends only 3 percent on overhead.

Most other industrial democracies use this type of low-overhead, tax-based public insurance system to cover all their citizens. They spend half of what we spend per person and they achieve better health outcomes. America wastes about 30 percent of our $2 trillion health care dollars on administration. Reducing administrative waste could save $300 billion each year, enough to cover all the uninsured and provide better coverage for the rest of us with complete choice of doctor and hospital.

Business owners stand to benefit, as well. A tax-financed, universal national health insurance system will help ensure a healthy workforce at a lower cost. Our current "non-system" is less effective at keeping workers healthy and productive, and its high costs reduce our competitiveness in the global marketplace.

America needs guaranteed, high-quality, affordable health insurance for all, with "everybody in and nobody out." We cannot attain this goal if we rely on schemes designed by Wall Street and the for-profit health insurance industry.

An improved and expanded Medicare for all is the proven cure and the only way to restore America's health. We can save lives, save money and make the right choice by supporting H.R. 676, the National Health Insurance Act.

"*The current healthcare system in this country has plenty of faults, but it's been proven time and again that there is no problem so grave that more government intervention can't make it even worse.*"

Medicare Is the Wrong Model for Reforming the U.S. Health Care System

William P. Hoar

In this viewpoint, William P. Hoar, a contributor to the New American, *argues that Medicare is not a suitable model for health care reform. While the author admits that health care in the U.S. has its faults, he claims that nationalizing health care would just make the problem worse. Supporters of this type of health care reform are using scare tactics to force their plan on the public, Hoar contends, and implementing the plan would result in the rationing of care, higher taxes, and job losses.*

William P. Hoar, "Washington Gives Us the Treatment," *New American*, August 31, 2009. Copyright © 2009 American Opinion Publishing Incorporated. Reproduced by permission.

As you read, consider the following questions:

1. According to President Barack Obama, if health care reform is not achieved, how many Americans will lose their health insurance each day?

2. What agencies does the author name as examples of government inefficiency?

3. According to the author, in what ways would people be negatively impacted by the proposed health care reforms?

If you ran across a mammoth sinkhole into which people were being forced to throw tax dollars—let's call it Medicare and note that the government itself says it faces bankruptcy in one short decade—would it occur to you to fix the situation by blasting that hole even deeper and coercing additional workers to shovel in greenbacks even faster? And then try to convince those doing the work that this would be a good way to save money?

Well, you might if you were the president or another supporter of nationalized healthcare. You might also blame the makers of the shovels for the situation in the same fashion the "evil" insurance industry is being portrayed as the villain in the current reform frenzy. Or you could try to shift the subject to those doing the shoveling, faulting them for being, say, too obese to fill in the pit caused by the explosion of mandated government spending.

The current healthcare system in this country has plenty of faults, but it's been proven time and again that there is no problem so grave that more government intervention can't make it even worse.

Scare Tactics

Searching for scapegoats, the president is calling out as scaremongers those who won't fall into line behind the passage of his hugely expensive legislation—costing the equivalent of the entire Brazilian economy. The bill being worked on in Washington runs to about a billion dollars a page—and represents more than the outlays of the entire U.S. government as late as 1986 or 1994 (depending on which of the shifting pieces of legislation are involved).

How is the president making his case? With well-reasoned facts? Nope. He's doing it by trying to frighten the bejabbers out of the public. The president has even charged that many doctors now perform tonsillectomies that aren't needed, presumably to drive up their payments. One gathers that this will change when bureaucrats are calling the shots.

Right after his railing against those advising caution, because, supposedly, those opposed to Obamacare are merely trying to scare the public, Obama himself resorted to scare tactics. If the nation fails to act, he divined, "I can almost guarantee you your premiums will double over the next 10 years," and you may not get a raise at your job to boot. The president keeps saying, for example: "If we do not reform health care, your premiums and out-of-pocket costs will continue to skyrocket. If we do not act, 14,000 Americans will continue to lose their health insurance every single day. These are the consequences of inaction." (Of course, Obama doesn't explain that the 14,000 "losing their health insurance" are mainly victims of other government malfeasance that has cratered the economy, such as job losses caused by government-subsidized immigrant workers and U.S. regulatory compliance costs that in 2006 were 31.7 percent higher than those of our nine largest trading partners.)

Problems with Nationalized Health Care

Yet, supporters of the president's reforms are advocating legislation that will tend to force employers away from providing healthcare benefits. Indeed, should you lose such benefits, the

Democrats have also proposed that you not be able to buy a new private policy because they want you in a public plan.

If you really want what amounts to a nationalized, government-run HMO, you'll love the Democrats' plans, which would lead to long lines, high costs, more taxes, and rationed care.

That is the considered view of many in the profession willing to look beyond the rhetoric in Washington. "This is war," commented George Watson, the president-elect of the Association of American Physicians and Surgeons. "This is a bureaucratic boondoggle to grab control of health care. Everything that has been proposed in the 1,018-page-bill will contribute to the ruination of medicine." The doctor noted that the legislation is crammed with rules and regulations that will result in shoddy care and lengthy waiting lines. A provision that would coerce doctors who contracted with Medicare into the nationalized plan is a "trap" that he compared to "involuntary servitude."

The White House disputes all of this of course. The president has praised the Mayo Clinic, among others, as a model for the nation, lauding its high-quality care "at costs well below the national norm." From his enthusiasm, you might think that his administration was itself responsible for such success. The reality is a bit different. "The Mayo Clinic and 12 other top health-care-delivery outlets just sent Congress a letter," wrote Grace-Marie Turner, president of the Galen Institute, in the *New York Post*, "warning that the bill that already has passed two committees in the House would put them out of business."

Do we really want healthcare run by those who have displayed the efficiency of the DMV and Postal Service and the compassion of the IRS? After all, the government already has a track record. Do we want to empower on a larger scale those who have been administering the long-suffering VA and Indian Health services and who have pushed Medicare and Medicaid to the brink of insolvency and beyond? Still, *Time* magazine asks plaintively in its recent cover story, "Can Obama Find a Cure?" as if the former community organizer were a medical research scientist on the verge of some grand discovery.

The government does not want true private competition. Indeed, ever-dependable columnist [Paul] Krugman declares it impossible to have free-market healthcare. Yet, the consequences of the proposed public alternative, in rather short order, would not be pretty. Writes Michael Cannon, director of health policies studies at the Cato Institute:

> After the Congressional Budget Office estimated that as many as 15 million Americans could lose their existing coverage under Senator Kennedy's legislation, the Associated Press reported, "White House officials suggest the president's rhetoric [about being able to keep your plan, no matter what] shouldn't be taken literally."
>
> Indeed, a new government program would literally oust millions of Americans from their current health plans and threaten their relationships with their doctors, as employers choose to drop their current employee health plans and as private health plans close down. A Lewin Group analysis estimated that Obama's campaign proposal would move 32 million Americans into a new government-run plan. Lewin subsequently estimated that if Congress used Medicare's price controls and opened the new program to everyone, it could pull 120 million Americans out of private insurance—more than half of the private market. The share of Americans who depend on government for their health care would rise from just over one-quarter to two-thirds.

Less Government, Not Big Government

The reformers have their eye fixed on more than bringing down the insurance industry. Big-government advocates literally want to run our lives—for our own good, of course. They are also willing to tax almost anything to herd us around as they so desire. Consider an all-too-typical example, from a healthcare blog in the *Los Angeles Times* for July 27 [2009]. The piece, called "Tough love for fat people: Tax their food to pay for healthcare," urged the United States to "adopt extensive menu- and food-labeling changes that would make 'good foods' easily distinguishable from the bad ones subject to added taxes. Not to worry though: Several European countries, most notably Great Britain, have led the way in this area."

Yes, that's the same no-so-great Britain where the Orwellian-nicknamed National Institute for Health and Clinical Excellence (NICE) board decides what treatments should be funded by the government based on an accounting statistic that measures, in terms of pounds, how much your life is worth.

Nevertheless, continued the *Los Angeles Times* do-gooder:

And here's the payoff: Conservatively estimated, a 10% tax levied on foods that would be defined as "less healthy" by a national standard adopted recently in Great Britain could yield $240 billion in its first five years and $522 billion over 10 years of implementation—if it were to begin in October 2010. If lawmakers instituted a program of tax subsidies to encourage the purchase of fresh and processed fruits and vegetables, the added revenue would still be $356 billion over 10 years.

Meanwhile, the legislation being foisted on the public has a lot in it other than what treatments you might be allowed. The Association of American Physicians and Surgeons has noted that there are even provisions for home visits that could provide parental counseling with Washington's wishes about "increasing birth intervals between pregnancies"—which probably translates quite easily into Chinese since it sounds suspiciously like Beijing's program.

Collectivism is key to Washington's legislative occupation of what should be personal business. Intrusive and expensive government, contrary to columnist Krugman, is actually behind virtually all of the ills of the system. As Sheldon Richman explained in an article for the Foundation for Economic Education:

> Nearly every aspect of medicine and health insurance that the politicians say needs fixing is the result of politicians' previous attempts to fix something. Much of the escalation of prices comes from consumer demand that is freed from normal cost constraints thanks to third-party payers: government-privileged insurance companies, Medicare, and Medicaid. While that intervention boosts demand by eliminating cost consciousness, others constrict supply: occupational licensing, insurance mandates and barriers to entry, patents on drugs and devices, FDA regulations, certificate-of-need requirements, and more.

> With each so-called reform, we (in reality, they, the politicians) made things worse. It's time we—collectively—stopped trying to reinvent the medical and insurance industries. Instead that task should be left to us individually—acting, transacting, competing, and cooperating in the marketplace. Only then will solutions emerge from people's—not politicians'—choices, as entrepreneurs (neither aided nor impeded by the State) pursue profit by producing goods and services that make us better off.

The reforms that are really needed involve less government, not more. Yet, the prescription being written for the United States by Dr. Obama and his congressional orderlies would insinuate Washington even deeper into healthcare matters. It would cost us in many ways. The added tax burden would be both direct and indirect. One method of financing in the House version of the legislation is what amounts to a jobs tax; the business levy would hurt those the reformers profess they want to help. Those workers who might "gain health insurance from ObamaCare," observed the *Wall Street Journal*, "will pay the steepest price for it in either a shrinking pay check, or no job at all."

That knock on the door is ominous; it's a snake-oil salesman from Washington who says he's got a cure-all. The government will simply lend a hand, we are told. We've been sold that bill of goods before. It is a mistake to believe, as proven by long, repeated, and painful experience, that Uncle Sam can open his wallet and let you keep yours closed.

> "*Universal coverage would stimulate the economy, it would boost the financial security of ordinary Americans, and it would break the health-care reform logjam.*"

The United States Should Move Rapidly to Implement Universal Health Care

Chris Farrell

In this viewpoint Chris Farrell, an economics editor for Busi-nessWeek and a frequent contributor to American Public Media's Marketplace Money, argues that implementing universal health care would be good for the U.S. economy. Universal health care should be implemented rapidly, as part of an economic stimulus package, even if adjustments to the plan are necessary later to create a more efficient system.

As you read, consider the following questions:

1. How much of the United States gross domestic product is spent on health, according to the author of this viewpoint?

Chris Farrell, "Want Real Stimulus? Try Universal Health Care," *BusinessWeek*, December 5, 2008. Copyright © 2008 by McGraw-Hill, Inc. Reproduced by permission.

2. How much does the author estimate that a universal health care program will cost?

3. Why does the author believe that health insurance should not be tied to employment?

The economy is in a tailspin. The latest salvo of grim tidings came courtesy of the Labor Dept.'s Dec. 5 employment report: U.S. employers slashed 533,000 jobs in November (BusinessWeek.com, 12/05/08), the largest monthly decline in more than three decades. The unemployment rate now stands at 6.7%, and the ranks of the jobless have increased by 2.7 million since December. The broadest measure of unemployment (a figure that includes the unemployed, employees laboring part-time, and others barely working) stands at a dismaying 12.5%, or 19.3 million workers, up from 8.4% a year ago, or 12.9 million workers.

Considering all the actions being taken by the U.S. Treasury and Federal Reserve to shore up the economy, the risk that a disinflationary recession deepens into a deflationary depression remains remote. But it isn't inconceivable.

The New Stimulus Package

To stave off an unwelcome reprise of the 1930s, the incoming Obama Administration and Congress are preparing a large fiscal stimulus package for the New Year. The centerpiece of the new Administration's initiative to get the economy going again was unveiled in news reports Dec. 6: The largest public works initiative since the creation of the national highway system in the late 1950s.

President-elect Obama highlighted the main components of the planned government investment in infrastructure: A massive effort to make public buildings more energy-efficient; more roads and bridges; upgrading school buildings; extending the information superhighway; and medical care electronic record keeping. It's increasingly apparent that the Detroit automakers will also get government money to stay alive.

Yet major health-care reform—specifically, universal health care—should top the list. Forget any suggestion that reform is too expensive or that it would take too long to have an impact. Wrong, on both counts. A bold embrace of universal health care offers policymakers the chance at a fiscal triple-play: Universal coverage would stimulate the economy, it would boost the financial security of ordinary Americans, and it would break the health-care reform log-jam.

Rx for a Healthy Economy

To paraphrase and update a famous quote about General Motors (GM), what's good for health-care reform is good for the economy. (It would certainly be good for General Motors, too.)

The case for long-term reform is compelling. The problems associated with America's badly frayed health-care system are well known. The country spends a world-beating 16% of gross domestic product on health, yet in international comparisons it lags behind a number of key measures. For instance, the U.S. ranks 29th in infant mortality and 48th in life expectancy. The number of people without health insurance was 38 million in 2007, and that number is guaranteed to have risen in the meantime with the recession that began a year ago. With universal health care, everyone under age 65 would be covered by a qualified health insurance company or through a government-sponsored program. (Those over 65 already have a version of universal coverage through Medicare.)

Universal coverage would boost the economy in the short term. The reason is that the financial side of the health-care equation is deteriorating rapidly for the average American family. Some 41% of working-age adults—72 million people— had trouble paying their medical bills or were paying off accrued medical debt from the past year. (That's up from 34%, or 58 million people, in 2005.) Taken altogether, in 2007 an estimated 116 million people, or two-thirds of working-age adults, were either uninsured for a time, faced steep out-of-pocket medical costs relative to their incomes, had difficulties paying their medical bills, or didn't get the care they needed ... according to the Commonwealth Fund Biennial Health Insurance Survey.

Targeting fiscal stimulus toward universal coverage would help ordinary workers rather than Wall Street tycoons. It would also relieve a major source of economic insecurity for anyone handed a pink slip during the recession.

Funding Health Care

For quick implementation, the initial system largely would take bigger and better advantage of existing programs. How much would it cost? Depending on the details, it would take somewhere between $100 billion and $200 billion to require that insurance companies abandon any screening based on preexisting conditions, fund tax credits for employers and workers, open up Medicare to younger folks, boost enrollment in State Children's Health Insurance Plans, and jump-start other initiatives to get everyone under the universal coverage umbrella.

Dean Baker, an economist and co-director of the Center for Economic & Policy Research has come up with a universal coverage package that would cost $160 billion a year. The main components of his idea: $120 billion in tax credits to employers who cover workers for the first time in 2009 and 2010, a credit for employers that increase their existing coverage, and another $40 billion to reduce the health-care burden on Medicare beneficiaries. (He would also open up Medicare to employers and individuals.)

What's more, rising health-care spending is not quite the devil it's often made out to be. The medical industry is among the nation's most globally competitive sectors. Health care is also a big U.S. employer, with 13.4 million workers. Indeed, even as most industries shrink their payrolls health care has created jobs. For instance, in November health-care employment grew by 34,000, and over the past 12 months the industry has added 369,000 jobs.

The Time Is Now

To be sure, this kind of universal health care isn't good enough for the long haul. It doesn't go far enough to create incentives for health-care efficiencies, let alone establish a stable source of funding. But once the economy recovers, Washington can debate how to create a more cost-effective and cost-efficient health-care system. Hopefully, any long-term solution will sever the link between health insurance and employment. It makes no sense that because a company's profits are down during a recession that a family's health-care coverage is at risk.

The country has toyed with some kind of national health policy six times over the past 100 years. A key plank in Theodore Roosevelt's losing Presidential campaign of 1912 was national health insurance. President Harry Truman tried again after World War II with his "Fair Deal." President Clinton's health-care initiative early in his first term collapsed. The current crisis offers another opportunity to reform the unwieldy, expensive apparatus at last—and give much needed relief to the beleaguered U.S. economy in the process.

> "The unsuccessful Clinton health plan was a political catastrophe for his party.... Were an Obama administration to fail similarly, the political consequences for the administration and the party could be equally serious."

The United States Should Move Forward Cautiously to Implement Universal Health Care

Henry J. Aaron

Henry J. Aaron, a senior fellow with the Brookings Institution, argues in this viewpoint that there is little chance that a universal health care bill can be successfully passed. Any attempt to do so would be seen as income redistribution and would evoke intense opposition. An attempt to pass a single encompassing universal health care bill would be politically dangerous for the Democrats and for President Barack Obama's administration.

Henry J. Aaron, "Healthy Choice: A Step-by-Step Approach to Universal Health Care," *The New Republic*, January 17, 2009. Copyright © 2009 by The New Republic, Inc. Reproduced by permission of The New Republic.

As you read, consider the following questions:

1. Why does the author of this viewpoint believe that the Democrats and the Obama administration might try to pass a single bill to implement universal health care at this time?

2. Why does the author believe it would be a mistake to attempt to pass a single bill to implement universal health care?

3. What is a health insurance clearinghouse, and why does the author believe it would be a good thing?

To many Democrats, it has long seemed self-evident that Barack Obama, if elected president, should promptly seek enactment of one big bill to achieve universal health insurance coverage and reform the U.S. health care system.

Senator Edward Kennedy is currently working with Senate colleagues to draft just such a bill. The appeal of this position is strong. Covering all Americans has been a goal of the Democratic Party for at least seventy years. Fifty million people remain uninsured. The quality of care in the U.S. is spotty, despite costs vastly greater than those of any other nation. Increasing outlays for Medicare and Medicaid threaten fiscal meltdown. Furthermore, candidate Obama campaigned on a program of sweeping reform—not, perhaps as comprehensive as those of his two major primary opponents, Hillary Clinton and John Edwards, but very large indeed. Many business executives, long opposed to government-led reform of health care financing, now clamor for government involvement. And the number of Democrats in both the House and the Senate is likely to increase. For all of these reasons, it is argued, now is the time!

Despite the appeal of swinging for the fences on health care reform, it would be a serious mistake for a President Obama to make sweeping reform an early first-term priority.

And the high cost of the current financial troubles is not the reason why. The fact is that a well executed "bailout" will not materially affect the long-term budget prospects of the federal government. Yes, it will initially boost spending and the national debt, but subsequent revenues from sale of acquired assets should offset those outlays. There are four other reasons why seeking to reform the whole health care system in one, large bill is unwise.

The Chances of Success Are Small. No consensus exists on how best to achieve universal coverage. Budget deficits that were foreseen before the bailout meant that no acceptable reform could substantially increase outlays, which requires that new spending—for example to cover the uninsured—must be offset by reduced spending for something else. The plain name for such spending shifts is income redistribution, the politics of which makes rugby scrums [fierce play] look positively gentlemanly. Resistance from those who are asked to pay more or receive less in the $2.6 trillion health care industry will be ferocious and well financed.

Recall that Democrats held 258 seats in the House (25 more than now and more than they are likely to hold in 2009) and 57 seats in the Senate (five more than now) when President [Bill] Clinton's health plan imploded. Right now, Democratic support is wobbly. On April 23, 2008, *The Hill* quoted Senator Jay Rockefeller saying: "We all know there is not enough money to do all this stuff"; Senator Charles Schumer saying: "Health care I feel strongly about, but I am not sure we're ready for a major national health care plan"; and Senator Max Baucus, chair of the key Committee on Finance: "If they try to solve all the problems, it's going to be difficult."

The Political Fallout from Failure Would Be Devastating. The unsuccessful Clinton health plan was a political catastrophe for his party. That failure was a major factor in the massive Democratic Party loss in the 1994 congressional election.

Were an Obama administration to fail similarly, the political consequences for the administration and the party could be equally serious.

Numerous Other Problems Cannot Wait. The next president will face an avalanche of issues neglected or mishandled by the [George W.] Bush administration. To the financial crisis, which is an obstacle more for the political energy that it will absorb than for its cost, add global warming, energy prices, Al Qaeda, Iraq, Iran, Afghanistan, the Arab-Israeli conflict, recession, income inequality, Social Security, rebuilding the U.S. military, and tax reform. To be sure, presidents always have to do many things at once, but their capacity to pursue major objectives simultaneously is severely limited. A failed effort to reform the U.S. health care system would not only generate direct political losses; it will also divert time and effort from other issues, some of which simply cannot wait or that offer greater opportunities for success than large-scale health care reform does.

The "Big Bang" Approach to Health Reform Is the Wrong Strategy. Congress is unlikely to change how the entire U.S. health care industry operates with one bill. And if it did so, it would probably make a hash [mess] of the job. The U.S. health care system is as large as the entire economy of France. Differences among the states in the cost and style of delivery of health care approximate those of the European Union. More importantly, apart from periods after major war or depression, democracies typically make large social and economic changes gradually, through laws enacted successively over many years.

So, rather than "betting the administration" on one shot, the sensible strategy would be to enunciate a broad vision for reform and propose practical steps to move in the envisioned direction. Get them through Congress, see what works and what doesn't, and then move forward again. Obama has already clearly articulated his vision. Here are four initial steps.

Steve Greenberg, *Ventura County Star (California)*, 2007.

Expand S-CHIP. Call upon Congress to once again pass the legislation President Bush vetoed that would have extended the State Child Health Insurance Program (S-CHIP) to an additional 5 million children. Though such legislation would not fully implement Senator Obama's promise to provide health insurance for every child, it would cover about 96 percent of them.

Start Testing Effectiveness. Earmark one percent of Medicare revenues and a similar share of private health care outlays to evaluating treatments and to establishing a national electronic database on medical outcomes. Most of the trillions spent on health care goes for services that have never been rigorously analyzed. The failure of the nation to invest in these studies is scandalous. Sensible cost control will remain nothing more than a topic of earnest conversation until information on what works and what does not work is available.

Encourage States' Efforts. Today, only Massachusetts has a comprehensive plan to extend coverage to the uninsured. Massachusetts is confronting—and, at least so far, solving—financial and administrative problems that any national program must address. If the federal government encouraged such state efforts, including some financial protection during economic slowdowns when state revenues drop and health spending does not, additional states would take the plunge, helping to pave the way for national legislation.

Create a National Health Insurance Clearing House. At a minimum, such an entity should regulate how health insurance is sold, so that buyers could easily compare features and prices. This inexpensive step would greatly improve the capacity of buyers to shop intelligently and encourage insurers to compete based on service. Massachusetts has created such an entity, called the Health Connector. Eventually, the clearing house could regulate health insurance prices, narrowing the huge variations that now make individual private insurance unaffordable for high-risk enrollees—the elderly and those with preexisting conditions. Over time, it could become a channel through which all or most people get coverage and that administers the subsidies that make insurance affordable.

No element of this program should face insuperable [unbeatable] legislative obstacles. The S-CHIP extension has already won majority support in Congress, failing only because of a presidential veto. The challenge to effectiveness research is less passing it than sustaining it when, as is inevitable, studies show that procedures, drugs, or devices backed by influential investors or practitioners are ineffective or excessively costly. To enable an agency to publish controversial findings and survive politically, the key is funding that is independent of annual appropriations and governance by directors appointed [for] lengthy, staggered terms and removable only for cause. Legislation to encourage state action already enjoys widespread bipartisan support—one House and two Senate bills have been introduced, all with bipartisan co-sponsorship— and would pass readily if backed by a popular president. The health insurance clearing house was spawned in a conservative think tank, but is an element of Senator Obama's campaign program.

These four reforms would not by themselves achieve universal coverage, end sub-standard care, or stop excessive growth of health care spending. But they would make material advances on all fronts and carry far less risk of political failure than the "big bang" approach. They would immediately increase the number of insured Americans by about ten million and set the stage for covering millions more. And they would provide information that will eventually make cost control possible and sustainable. Democrats should beware of once again approaching health care reform the way [in the comic strip *Peanuts*] Charlie Brown always approached the football that Lucy held—heedless of experience, credulously hopeful, and flat on their backs.

"We cannot swap out our old system for a new one. . . . But we can construct a kind of lifeboat alongside it for those who have been left out or dumped out."

The United States Can Achieve Universal Health Care Without Dismantling the Existing Health Care System

Atul Gawande

In this viewpoint Atul Gawande, a physician and professor of surgery and public health at Harvard University, and a staff writer for the New Yorker *magazine, draws on the history of universal health care in Great Britain, France, and Switzerland to argue that the United States can implement universal health care by building on existing programs such as the Department of Veteran Affairs hospital system and Medicare, while leaving the existing private insurance program in place.*

As you read, consider the following questions:

1. According to the author of this viewpoint, Great Britain developed its universal health care program during World War II, to cope with a crisis, and did not intend for it to become permanent. What happened that led the country to implement the National Health Service as a permanent program in 1945?

2. The author considers a universal health care program as a "lifeboat" alongside the present health care system "for those who have been left out or dumped out." What does he mean by this?

3. The author describes efforts to implement universal health care in the state of Massachusetts. What changes did the state make in 2007 in order to make private health insurance available to everyone?

In every industrialized nation, the movement to reform health care has begun with stories about cruelty. The Canadians had stories like the 1946 Toronto *Globe and Mail* report of a woman in labor who was refused help by three successive physicians, apparently because of her inability to pay. In Australia, a 1954 letter published in the Sydney *Morning Herald* sought help for a young woman who had lung disease. She couldn't afford to refill her oxygen tank, and had been forced to ration her intake "to a point where she is on the borderline of death." In Britain, George Bernard Shaw was at a London hospital visiting an eminent physician when an assistant came in to report that a sick man had arrived requesting treatment. "Is he worth it?" the physician asked. It was the normality of the question that shocked Shaw and prompted his scathing and influential 1906 play, "The Doctor's Dilemma." The British health system, he charged, was "a conspiracy to exploit popular credulity and human suffering."

In the United States, our stories are like the one that appeared in the *Times* before Christmas. Starla Darling, pregnant and due for delivery, had just taken maternity leave from her factory job at Archway & Mother's Cookie Company, in Ashland, Ohio, when she received a letter informing her that the company was going out of business. In three days, the letter said, she and almost three hundred co-workers would be laid off, and would lose their health-insurance coverage. The company was self-insured, so the employees didn't have the option of paying for the insurance themselves—their insurance plan was being terminated.

"When I heard that I was losing my insurance, I was scared," Darling told the *Times*. Her husband had been laid off from his job, too. "I remember that the bill for my son's delivery in 2005 was about $9,000, and I knew I would never be able to pay that by myself." So she prevailed on her midwife to induce labor while she still had insurance coverage. During labor, Darling began bleeding profusely, and needed a Cesarean section. Mother and baby pulled through. But the insurer denied Darling's claim for coverage. The couple ended up owing more than seventeen thousand dollars.

The stories become unconscionable in any society that purports to serve the needs of ordinary people, and, at some alchemical point, they combine with opportunity and leadership to produce change. Britain reached this point and enacted universal health-care coverage in 1945, Canada in 1966, Australia in 1974. The United States may finally be there now. In 2007, fifty-seven million Americans had difficulty paying their medical bills, up fourteen million from 2003. On average, they had two thousand dollars in medical debt and had been contacted by a collection agency at least once. Because, in part, of underpayment, half of American hospitals operated at a loss in 2007. Today, large numbers of employers are limiting or dropping insurance coverage in order to stay afloat, or simply going under—even hospitals themselves.

Yet wherever the prospect of universal health insurance has been considered, it has been widely attacked as a Bolshevik fantasy—a coercive system to be imposed upon people by benighted socialist master planners. People fear the unintended consequences of drastic change, the blunt force of government. However terrible the system may seem, we all know that it could be worse—especially for those who already have dependable coverage and access to good doctors and hospitals.

Many would-be reformers hold that "true" reform must simply override those fears. They believe that a new system will be far better for most people, and that those who would hang on to the old do so out of either lack of imagination or narrow self-interest. On the left, then, single-payer enthusiasts argue that the only coherent solution is to end private health insurance and replace it with a national insurance program. And, on the right, the free marketeers argue that the only coherent solution is to end public insurance and employer-controlled health benefits so that we can all buy our own coverage and put market forces to work.

Neither side can stand the other. But both reserve special contempt for the pragmatists, who would build around the mess we have. The country has this one chance, the idealist maintains, to sweep away our inhumane, wasteful patchwork system and replace it with something new and more rational. So we should prepare for a bold overhaul, just as every other Western democracy has. True reform requires transformation at a stroke. But is this really the way it has occurred in other countries? The answer is no. And the reality of how health reform has come about elsewhere is both surprising and instructive.

No example is more striking than that of Great Britain, which has the most socialized health system in the industrialized world. Established on July 5, 1948, the National Health Service owns the vast majority of the country's hospitals, blood banks, and ambulance operations, employs most specialist physicians as salaried government workers, and has made medical care available to every resident for free. The system is so thoroughly government-controlled that, across the Atlantic, we imagine it had to have been imposed by fiat, by the coercion of ideological planners bending the system to their will.

But look at the news report in the *Times* of London on July 6, 1948, headlined "FIRST DAY OF HEALTH SERVICE." You might expect descriptions of bureaucratic shock troops walking into hospitals, insurance-company executives and doctors protesting in the streets, patients standing outside chemist shops worrying about whether they can get their prescriptions filled. Instead, there was only a four-paragraph notice between an item on the King and Queen's return from a holiday in Scotland and one on currency problems in Germany.

The beginning of the new national health service "was taking place smoothly," the report said. No major problems were noted by the 2,751 hospitals involved or by patients arriving to see their family doctors. Ninety per cent of the British Medical Association's members signed up with the program voluntarily—and found that they had a larger and steadier income by doing so. The greatest difficulty, it turned out, was the unexpected pent-up demand for everything from basic dental care to pediatric visits for hundreds of thousands of people who had been going without.

The program proved successful and lasting, historians say, precisely because it was not the result of an ideologue's master plan. Instead, the N.H.S. was a pragmatic outgrowth of circumstances peculiar to Britain immediately after the Second World War. The single most important moment that determined what Britain's health-care system would look like was not any policymaker's meeting in 1945 but the country's declaration of war on Germany, on September 3, 1939.

As tensions between the two countries mounted, Britain's ministers realized that they would have to prepare not only for land and sea combat but also for air attacks on cities on an unprecedented scale. And so, in the days before war was declared, the British government oversaw an immense evacuation; three and a half million people moved out of the cities and into the countryside. The government had to arrange transport and lodging for those in need, along with supervision, food, and schooling for hundreds of thousands of children whose parents had stayed behind to join in the war effort. It also had to insure that medical services were in place—both in the receiving regions, whose populations had exploded, and in the cities, where up to two million war-injured civilians and returning servicemen were anticipated.

As a matter of wartime necessity, the government began a national Emergency Medical Service to supplement the local services. Within a period of months, sometimes weeks, it built or expanded hundreds of hospitals. It conducted a survey of the existing hospitals and discovered that essential services were either missing or severely inadequate—laboratories, X-ray facilities, ambulances, care for fractures and burns and head injuries. The Ministry of Health was forced to upgrade and, ultimately, to operate these services itself.

The war compelled the government to provide free hospital treatment for civilian casualties, as well as for combatants. In London and other cities, the government asked local hospitals to transfer some of the sick to private hospitals in the outer suburbs in order to make room for victims of the war. As a result, the government wound up paying for a large fraction of the private hospitals' costs. Likewise, doctors received government salaries for the portion of their time that was devoted to the new wartime medical service. When the Blitz came, in September, 1940, vast numbers of private hospitals and clinics were destroyed, further increasing the government's share of medical costs. The private hospitals and doctors whose doors were still open had far fewer paying patients and were close to financial ruin.

Churchill's government intended the program to be temporary. But the war destroyed the status quo for patients, doctors, and hospitals alike. Moreover, the new system proved better than the old. Despite the ravages of war, the health of the population had improved. The medical and social services had reduced infant and adult mortality rates. Even the dental care was better. By the end of 1944, when the wartime medical service began to demobilize, the country's citizens did not want to see it go. The private hospitals didn't, either; they had come to depend on those government payments.

By 1945, when the National Health Service was proposed, it had become evident that a national system of health coverage was not only necessary but also largely already in place—with nationally run hospitals, salaried doctors, and free care for everyone. So, while the ideal of universal coverage was spurred by those horror stories, the particular system that emerged in Britain was not the product of socialist ideology or a deliberate policy process in which all the theoretical options were weighed. It was, instead, an almost conservative creation: a program that built on a tested, practical means of providing adequate health care for everyone, while protecting the existing services that people depended upon every day. No other major country has adopted the British system—not because it didn't work but because other countries came to universalize health care under entirely different circumstances.

In France, in the winter of 1945, President [Charles] de Gaulle was likewise weighing how to insure that his nation's population had decent health care after the devastation of war. But the system that he inherited upon liberation had no significant public insurance or hospital sector. Seventy-five per cent of the population paid cash for private medical care, and many people had become too destitute to afford heat, let alone medications or hospital visits.

Long before the war, large manufacturers and unions had organized collective insurance funds for their employees, financed through a self-imposed payroll tax, rather than a set premium. This was virtually the only insurance system in place, and it became the scaffolding for French health care. With an almost impossible range of crises on its hands—food shortages, destroyed power plants, a quarter of the population living as refugees—the de Gaulle government had neither the time nor the capacity to create an entirely new health-care system. So it built on what it had, expanding the existing payroll-tax-funded, private insurance system to cover all wage earners, their families, and retirees. The self-employed were added in the nineteen-sixties. And the remainder of uninsured residents were finally included in 2000.

Today, Sécurité Sociale provides payroll-tax-financed insurance to all French residents, primarily through a hundred and forty-four independent, not-for-profit, local insurance funds. The French health-care system has among the highest public-satisfaction levels of any major Western country; and, compared with Americans, the French have a higher life expectancy, lower infant mortality, more physicians, and lower costs. In 2000, the World Health Organization ranked it the best health-care system in the world. (The United States was ranked thirty-seventh.)

Switzerland, because of its wartime neutrality, escaped the damage that drove health-care reform elsewhere.

Instead, most of its citizens came to rely on private commercial health-insurance coverage. When problems with coverage gaps and inconsistencies finally led the nation to pass its universal-coverage law, in 1994, it had no experience with public insurance. So the country—you get the picture now—built on what it already had. It required every resident to purchase private health insurance and provided subsidies to limit the cost to no more than about ten percent of an individual's income.

Every industrialized nation in the world except the United States has a national system that guarantees affordable health care for all its citizens. Nearly all have been popular and successful. But each has taken a drastically different form, and the reason has rarely been ideology. Rather, each country has built on its own history, however imperfect, unusual, and untidy.

Social scientists have a name for this pattern of evolution based on past experience. They call it "path-dependence." In the battles between Betamax and VHS video recorders, Mac and P.C. computers, the QWERTY typewriter keyboard and alternative designs, they found that small, early events played a far more critical role in the market outcome than did the question of which design was better. Paul Krugman received a Nobel Prize in Economics in part for showing that trade patterns and the geographic location of industrial production are also path-dependent. The first firms to get established in a given industry, he pointed out, attract suppliers, skilled labor, specialized financing, and physical infrastructure. This entrenches local advantages that lead other firms producing similar goods to set up business in the same area—even if prices, taxes, and competition are stiffer. "The long shadow cast by history over location is apparent at all scales, from the smallest to the largest—from the cluster of costume jewelry firms in Providence to the concentration of 60 million people in the Northeast Corridor," Krugman wrote in 1991.

With path-dependent processes, the outcome is unpredictable at the start. Small, often random events early in the process are "remembered," continuing to have influence later. And, as you go along, the range of future possibilities gets narrower. It becomes more and more unlikely that you can simply shift from one path to another, even if you are locked in on a path that has a lower payoff than an alternate one.

The political scientist Paul Pierson observed that this sounds a lot like politics, and not just economics. When a social policy entails major setup costs and large numbers of people who must devote time and resources to developing expertise, early choices become difficult to reverse. And if the choices involve what economists call "increasing returns"—where the benefits of a policy increase as more people organize their activities around it—those early decisions become self-reinforcing. America's transportation system developed this way. The century-old decision to base it on gasoline-powered automobiles led to a gigantic manufacturing capacity, along with roads, repair facilities, and fuelling stations that now make it exceedingly difficult to do things differently.

There's a similar explanation for our employment-based health-care system. Like Switzerland, America made it through the war without damage to its domestic infrastructure. Unlike Switzerland, we sent much of our workforce abroad to fight. This led the Roosevelt Administration to impose national wage controls to prevent inflationary increases in labor costs. Employers who wanted to compete for workers could, however, offer commercial health insurance. That spurred our distinctive reliance on private insurance obtained through one's place of employment—a source of troubles (for employers and the unemployed alike) that we've struggled with for six decades.

Some people regard the path-dependence of our policies as evidence of weak leadership; we have, they charge, allowed our choices to be constrained by history and by vested interests. But that's too simple. The reality is that leaders are held responsible for the hazards of change as well as for the benefits. And the history of master-planned transformation isn't exactly inspiring. The familiar horror story is Mao's Great Leap Forward, where the collectivization of farming caused some thirty million deaths from famine. But, to take an example from our own era, consider Defense Secretary Donald Rumsfeld's disastrous reinvention of modern military operations for the 2003 invasion of Iraq, in which he insisted on deploying far fewer ground troops than were needed. Or consider a health-care example: the 2003 prescription-drug program for America's elderly.

This legislation aimed to expand the Medicare insurance program in order to provide drug coverage for some ten million elderly Americans who lacked it, averaging fifteen hundred dollars per person annually. The White House, congressional Republicans, and the pharmaceutical industry opposed providing this coverage through the existing Medicare public-insurance program. Instead, they created an entirely new, market-oriented program that offered the elderly an online choice of competing, partially subsidized commercial drug-insurance plans. It was, in theory, a reasonable approach. But it meant that twenty-five million Americans got new drug plans, and that all sixty thousand retail pharmacies in the United States had to establish contracts and billing systems for those plans.

On January 1, 2006, the program went into effect nationwide. The result was chaos. There had been little realistic consideration of how millions of elderly people with cognitive difficulties, chronic illness, or limited English would manage to select the right plan for themselves. Even the savviest struggled to figure out how to navigate the choices: insurance companies offered 1,429 prescription-drug plans across the country. People arrived at their pharmacy only to discover that they needed an insurance card that hadn't come, or that they hadn't received pre-authorization for their drugs, or had switched to a plan that didn't cover the drugs they took. Tens of thousands were unable to get their prescriptions filled, many for essential drugs like insulin, inhalers, and blood-pressure medications. The result was a public-health crisis in thirty-seven states, which had to provide emergency pharmacy payments for the frail. We will never know how many were harmed, but it is likely that the program killed people.

This is the trouble with the lure of the ideal. Over and over in the health-reform debate, one hears serious policy analysts say that the only genuine solution is to replace our health-care system (with a single-payer system, a free-market system, or whatever); anything else is a missed opportunity. But this is a siren song.

Yes, American health care is an appallingly patched-together ship, with rotting timbers, water leaking in, mercenaries on board, and fifteen per cent of the passengers thrown over the rails just to keep it afloat. But hundreds of millions of people depend on it. The system provides more than thirty-five million hospital stays a year, sixty-four million surgical procedures, nine hundred million office visits, three and a half billion prescriptions. It represents a sixth of our economy. There is no dry-docking health care for a few months, or even for an afternoon, while we rebuild it. Grand plans admit no possibility of mistakes or failures, or the chance to learn from them. If we get things wrong, people will die. This doesn't mean that ambitious reform is beyond us. But we have to start with what we have.

That kind of constraint isn't unique to the health-care system. A century ago, the modern phone system was built on a structure that came to be called the P.S.T.N., the Public Switched Telephone Network. This automated system connects our phone calls twenty-four hours a day, and over time it has had to be upgraded. But you can't turn off the phone system and do a reboot. It's too critical to too many. So engineers have had to add on one patch after another.

The P.S.T.N. is probably the shaggiest, most convoluted system around; it contains tens of millions of lines of software code. Given a chance for a do-over, no self-respecting engineer would create anything remotely like it. Yet this jerry-rigged system has provided us with 911 emergency service, voice mail, instant global connectivity, mobile-phone lines, and the transformation from analog to digital communication. It has also been fantastically reliable, designed to have as little as two hours of total downtime every forty years. As a system that can't be turned off, the P.S.T.N. may be the ultimate in path-dependence. But that hasn't prevented dramatic change. The structure may not have undergone revolution; the way it functions has. The P.S.T.N. has made the twenty-first century possible.

So accepting the path-dependent nature of our health-care system—recognizing that we had better build on what we've got—doesn't mean that we have to curtail our ambitions. The overarching goal of health-care reform is to establish a system that has three basic attributes. It should leave no one uncovered—medical debt must disappear as a cause of personal bankruptcy in America. It should no longer be an economic catastrophe for employers. And it should hold doctors, nurses, hospitals, drug and device companies, and insurers collectively responsible for making care better, safer, and less costly.

We cannot swap out our old system for a new one that will accomplish all this. But we can build a new system on the old one. On the start date for our new health-care system— on, say, January 1, 2011—there need be no noticeable change for the vast majority of Americans who have dependable coverage and decent health care. But we can construct a kind of lifeboat alongside it for those who have been left out or dumped out, a rescue program for people like Starla Darling.

In designing this program, we'll inevitably want to build on the institutions we already have. That precept sounds as if it would severely limit our choices. But our health-care system has been a hodgepodge for so long that we actually have experience with all kinds of systems. The truth is that American health care has been more flotilla than ship. Our veterans' health-care system is a program of twelve hundred government-run hospitals and other medical facilities all across the country (just like Britain's). We could open it up to other people. We could give people a chance to join Medicare, our government insurance program (much like Canada's). Or we could provide people with coverage through the benefits program that federal workers already have, a system of private-insurance choices (like Switzerland's).

These are all established programs, each with advantages and disadvantages. The veterans' system has low costs, one of the nation's best information-technology systems for health care, and quality of care that (despite what you've heard) has, in recent years, come to exceed the private sector's on numerous measures. But it has a tightly limited choice of clinicians—you can't go to see any doctor you want, and the nearest facility may be far away from where you live. Medicare allows you to go to almost any private doctor or hospital you like, and has been enormously popular among its beneficiaries, but it costs about a third more per person and has had a hard time getting doctors and hospitals to improve the quality and safety of their care. Federal workers are entitled to a range of subsidized private-insurance choices, but insurance companies have done even less than Medicare to contain costs and most have done little to improve health care (although there are some striking exceptions).

Any of the programs could allow us to offer a starting group of Americans—the uninsured under twenty-five years of age, say—the chance to join within weeks. With time and experience, the programs could be made available to everyone who lacks coverage. The current discussion between the Obama Administration and congressional leaders seems to center on opening up the federal workers' insurance options *and* Medicare (or the equivalent) this way, with subsidized premiums for those with low incomes. The costs have to be dealt with. The leading proposals would try to hold down health-care spending in various ways (by, for example, requiring better management of patients with expensive chronic diseases); employers would have to pay some additional amount in taxes if they didn't provide health insurance for their employees. There's nothing easy about any of this. But, if we accept it, we'll all have a lifeboat when we need one.

It won't necessarily be clear what the final system will look like. Maybe employers will continue to slough off benefits, and that lifeboat will grow to become the entire system. Or maybe employers will decide to strengthen their benefits programs to attract employees, and American health care will emerge as a mixture of the new and the old. We could have Medicare for retirees, the V.A. for veterans, employer-organized insurance for some workers, federally organized insurance for others. The system will undoubtedly be messier than anything an idealist would devise. But the results would almost certainly be better.

Massachusetts, where I live and work, recently became the first state to adopt a system of universal health coverage for its residents. It didn't organize a government takeover of the state's hospitals or insurance companies, or force people into a new system of state-run clinics. It built on what existed. On July 1, 2007, the state began offering an online choice of four private insurance plans for people without health coverage. The cost is zero for the poor; for the rest, it is limited to no more than about eight per cent of income. The vast majority of families, who had insurance through work, didn't notice a thing when the program was launched. But those who had no coverage had to enroll in a plan or incur a tax penalty.

The results have been remarkable. After a year, 97.4 per cent of Massachusetts residents had coverage, and the remaining gap continues to close. Despite the requirement that individuals buy insurance and that employers either provide coverage or pay a tax, the program has remained extremely popular. Repeated surveys have found that at least two-thirds of the state's residents support the reform.

The Massachusetts plan didn't do anything about medical costs, however, and, with layoffs accelerating, more people require subsidized care than the state predicted. Insurance premiums continue to rise here, just as they do elsewhere in the country. Many residents also complain that eight per cent of their income is too much to pay for health insurance, even though, on average, premiums amount to twice that much. The experience has shown national policymakers that they will have to be serious about reducing costs.

For all that, the majority of state residents would not go back to the old system. I'm among them. For years, about one in ten of my patients—I specialize in cancer surgery—had no insurance. Even though I'd waive my fee, they struggled to pay for their tests, medications, and hospital stay.

I once took care of a nineteen-year-old college student who had maxed out her insurance coverage. She had a treatable but metastatic cancer. But neither she nor her parents could afford the radiation therapy that she required. I made calls to find state programs, charities—anything that could help her—to no avail. She put off the treatment for almost a year because she didn't want to force her parents to take out a second mortgage on their home. But eventually they had to choose between their daughter and their life's savings.

For the past year, I haven't had a single Massachusetts patient who has had to ask how much the necessary tests will cost; not one who has told me he needed to put off his cancer operation until he found a job that provided insurance coverage. And that's a remarkable change: a glimpse of American health care without the routine cruelty.

It will be no utopia. People will still face co-payments and premiums. There may still be agonizing disputes over coverage for non-standard treatments. Whatever the system's contours, we will still find it exasperating, even disappointing. We're not going to get perfection. But we can have transformation— which is to say, a health-care system that works. And there are ways to get there that start from where we are.

> *"The single biggest source of medical re-*
> *search funding . . . is the National In-*
> *stitutes of Health (NIH). . . . There's no*
> *reason why this has to change under*
> *universal health insurance."*

It Is Possible for the United States to Achieve Universal Health Care While Protecting Scientific Innovation

Jonathan Cohn

Jonathan Cohn, a senior editor at the New Republic *magazine,*
addresses a frequent criticism of universal health care plans—
that they would destroy free-market incentives for scientific in-
novation that drive the American health care system. Cohn ar-
gues that the U.S. edge in medical innovation is not due to
spending by the private insurance sector, but rather to the
nation's funding of the National Institutes of Health, which sup-
ports research in academic settings. The U.S. commitment to
medical research through the NIH would not have to change
with the implementation of universal health care.

Jonathan Cohn, "Creative Destruction: The Best Case Against Universal Health Care,"
The New Republic, November 12, 2007. Copyright © 2007 by The New Republic, Inc.
Reproduced by permission of The New Republic.

As you read, consider the following questions:

1. The author begins by telling a story about a colleague's illness, which was treated with a procedure called DBS, or Deep Brain Stimulation. Why does the author think the story about the development of DBS is important?

2. According to the author, do most medical breakthroughs take place in academia or in the private sector?

3. The author notes that funding for the National Institutes of Health (NIH) decreased under the George W. Bush administration. How does decreased funding of the NIH affect medical research?

More than a decade ago, Michael Kinsley, the journalist and former editor of this magazine, developed Parkinson's disease—a degenerative condition that impairs motor and speech control, producing tremors, rigidity, and eventually severe disability. While the standard regimen of medications helped, he knew that his symptoms were bound to get steadily worse with time. He needed something better—something innovative—before the disease really progressed. In 2006, he got it at the famed Cleveland Clinic in Ohio.

The treatment Mike received is called Deep Brain Stimulation, or DBS for short. It began with a physician—one of the world's top Parkinson's specialists—drilling two holes in his head, into which were implanted two thin electrodes made of titanium. The electrodes were attached to wires, which the physician threaded behind the internal portions of Mike's ear, down his neck, and eventually into his chest cavity, where they were connected to a pair of tiny battery-powered controllers. After the surgery, the doctor activated the controllers using a remote device, unleashing a steady pulse of small electrical shocks that ran across the wires, through the electrodes, and—finally—to the part of the brain that regulates movement. DBS doesn't cure Parkinson's, but it has been shown to control the symptoms for extended periods of time. And that's what happened for Mike (who is also, full disclosure, a friend).

A Costly Cutting-Edge Treatment

DBS represents the cutting edge of Parkinson's treatment; the Food and Drug Administration approved it only ten years ago. It is also very costly. Medtronic, a company that makes the electrodes, says the whole procedure costs between $50,000 and $60,000. And, because the treatment's main effect is to suppress and delay the onset of symptoms, rather than cure the disease, Mike started wondering whether a system of universal health insurance would pay for it—and, if so, in which cases.

After all, in universal coverage systems, the government typically defines a minimum set of benefits—a list that is put together based on frank assessments of cost effectiveness. (Even if the government achieves universal coverage through private plans rather than through a single-payer system, most insurers would likely end up offering something very close to that same set of benefits.) The government might decide that $50,000 or $60,000 is simply too much to spend for something that doesn't cure Parkinson's—or, at least, limit the treatment to certain people, such as those in more advanced stages of the disease. Mike could always have paid for the procedure out of his own pocket. But most Americans couldn't. If the government decided the treatment wasn't cost effective, he pointed out, many Americans would be forced to go without it—unless they could find a doctor and hospital willing to do it for free.

And that prompted another thought—not from Mike but from me. All of this was assuming DBS even existed. The United States is famously the world leader in medical innovation—in part, it would seem, because we spend like a drunken sailor when it comes to medical care. Today, we devote 16 percent of our gross domestic product to health care, by far the largest proportion of any country in the world. (The highest spending country in Europe, Switzerland, devotes just 12 percent.) That huge, largely uncontrolled spending translates into large profits for health care companies, offering an incentive for them to do research and development—the kind, presumably, that plays a significant role in breakthroughs like DBS. Universal health care would attempt to bring health care costs under control by, among other things, using government's leverage to drive down prices of everything from medical services to drugs and devices. And, if the payoff for something like DBS weren't as big as it is now, who's to say a company would have bothered developing it in the first place?

As Mike himself acknowledged, none of this seals the case against universal health care. On the contrary, maybe the trade-offs between covering everybody and fostering innovative health care are inevitable—and perhaps innovation has to come second. Maybe what is good for some people with Parkinson's isn't necessarily in the best interests of the country as a whole. On the other hand, people with Parkinson's can contribute more to the economy (and society in general) if their symptoms subside. They might also need less ongoing care, which could actually save money. Besides, true innovation ultimately benefits everybody by pushing the boundaries of the medically possible. Can we really count on a universal coverage system to weigh all of that? In other words, can we really be sure that universal health care won't come at the expense of innovative medicine?

Would Innovation Thrive Under Universal Health Care?

It's a valid set of questions, which is more than you can say for most of the arguments against universal health care circulating these days. If you've listened to Rudy Giuliani or any of the other Republican presidential candidates [for the 2008 election] lately, then you've probably heard them claim that creating universal health care would necessarily lead to inferior treatments, particularly for deadly diseases like cancer. But that just isn't so. While the United States is a world leader in cancer care, other countries, such as France, Sweden, and Switzerland, boast overall survival rates that are nearly comparable. For some variants—such as cervical cancer, non-Hodgkin lymphoma, and two common forms of leukemia—the U.S. survival rate, although good, lags behind at least some other countries. You may also have heard critics complain that universal health care inevitably leads to long lines for treatments, as it sometimes has in Britain and Canada. Again, the facts just don't back that up. According to the Organization for Economic Cooperation and Development, France and Germany don't have chronic waiting lines. Access to care in those countries turns out to be as easy as, if not easier than, in the United States, where even people with good private insurance must sometimes wait to see a specialist or go through managed care gatekeepers to get tests and treatments recommended by their physicians. As *National Review*'s Ramesh Ponnuru recently acknowledged, in a refreshing burst of candor, "[T]he best national health-insurance programs do not bear out the horror stories that conservatives like to tell about them."

But one argument against universal health insurance isn't so easy to dismiss: the argument about innovation and the cutting edge of medical care. It goes more or less along the lines of my conversation with Mike Kinsley: In a universal coverage system, the government would seek to limit spending by forcing down payments to doctors and pharmaceutical companies, while scrutinizing treatments for cost-effectiveness. This, in turn, would lead to both less innovation and less access to the innovation that already exists. And the public would end up losing out, because, as Tyler Cowen wrote last year in the *New York Times*, "the American health care system, high expenditures and all, is driving innovation for the entire world."

Cowen, a George Mason University economist, is a self-described libertarian. But it's not just libertarians, or even just conservatives, who say such things. Liberals have been known to voice similar concerns, albeit more carefully. Notable among them is David Cutler, a highly respected Harvard economist, whose book *Your Money or Your Life* makes a powerful argument that spending a lot of money on health care is frequently worth it—specifically, that investments in areas like neonatal and cardiovascular care have produced longer and healthier lives, more than justifying their exorbitant price tags. And, while Cutler's work on this subject remains somewhat iconoclastic, most economists would concede that it's possible a universal system could stifle innovation by pushing too hard on prices or applying the wrong kind of scrutiny to medical treatments.

But it's one thing to say that universal coverage *could* lead to less innovation or reduce the availability of high-tech care. It is quite another to say that it *will* do those things, which is the claim that opponents frequently make. That argument requires several leaps of logic, many of them highly suspect. The forces that produce innovation in medicine turn out to be a great deal more complicated than critics of universal coverage seem to grasp. Ultimately, whether innovation would continue to thrive under universal health care depends entirely on what kind of system we create and how well we run it. In fact, it's quite possible that universal coverage could lead to *better* innovation.

Lessons in Innovation

The story of Deep Brain Stimulation actually holds some important lessons about how innovation frequently takes place—and why it's not all that dependent on a non-universal, private health care system like the one we have in the United States. For one thing, it turns out that DBS isn't exactly an American

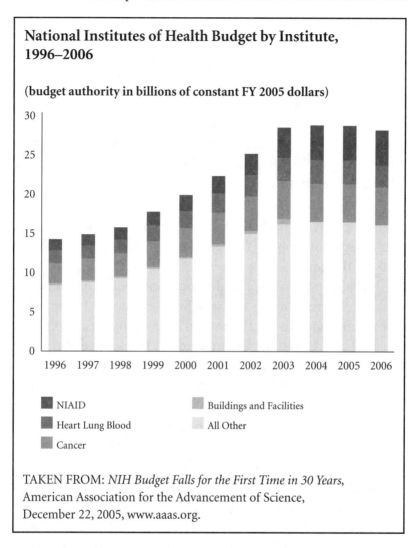

National Institutes of Health Budget by Institute, 1996–2006

(budget authority in billions of constant FY 2005 dollars)

- NIAID
- Heart Lung Blood
- Cancer
- Buildings and Facilities
- All Other

TAKEN FROM: *NIH Budget Falls for the First Time in 30 Years,* American Association for the Advancement of Science, December 22, 2005, www.aaas.org.

innovation. If anybody deserves credit for developing it, it's the French—and one French doctor in particular.

That doctor's name is Alim-Louis Benabid. A recently retired neurosurgeon who did his work at the University of Grenoble, near the French Alps, Benabid spent the early part of his career treating Parkinson's patients with what was, at the time, the standard regimen: first, medication; then, when the medication stopped working, surgery. The surgery involved performing lesions in the brain—that is, deliberately damaging or removing diseased tissue—with the hope of destroying the part that was causing the tremors and disability. This procedure sometimes alleviated symptoms, but it was also a clumsy, irreversible move with the potential for severe side-effects. (It was easy to damage the wrong part of the brain.) That's why it was reserved for patients with the worst symptoms—those for whom medication had either stopped working or never worked at all.

The key challenge in surgery was always figuring out where, exactly, to perform the lesions. To do that, surgeons would begin by applying small electrical charges to different parts of the brain—then observe which part of the body reacted. (Patients were kept under local anesthesia only, so their bodies could respond to the stimuli.) Benabid was doing that to a patient one day in 1985 when serendipity struck: One of the shocks suddenly caused a tremor to stop altogether. As he later explained in an interview with *Technology Review*, Benabid at first thought he had hurt the patient and apologized. But the patient said, "No, no, it was nice." So Benabid tried again—and, once again, the charge stopped the tremor. "My first thought was, I was relieved it wasn't a complication. The concomitant thought was, 'That's interesting!'"

Benabid theorized that applying a charge on a constant basis might suppress symptoms for long periods of time. And a prototype of hardware for doing that already existed: Years before, neurosurgeons had begun using small implanted electrodes to treat severe chronic pain, such as the kind that often followed a stroke. Benabid began experimenting in 1987 with the use of electrodes in Parkinson's patients and, in 1996, published what is now considered the seminal paper demonstrating that DBS can work.

The development of DBS was one part basic knowledge—an understanding of how Parkinson's works and how the brain responds to electrical stimulation—and one part sheer luck. Profits, on the other hand, had relatively little to do with it. According to Robert Gross, an Emory University neurosurgeon and expert in the field, Benabid had actually approached the companies that already made electrodes for use in treating chronic pain, suggesting they develop a device specifically for Parkinson's. But they declined initially, so Benabid had to use the existing devices and adapt them on his own. "The companies did not lead those advances," Gross says. "They followed them."

How Innovation Really Happens

In this sense, DBS offers an important window into the way medical innovation actually happens. The great breakthroughs in the history of medicine, from the development of the polio vaccine to the identification of cancer-killing agents, did not take place because a for-profit company saw an opportunity and invested heavily in research. They happened because of scientists toiling in academic settings. "The nice thing about people like me in universities is that the great majority are not motivated by profit," says Cynthia Kenyon, a renowned cancer researcher at the University of California at San Francisco. "If we were, we wouldn't be here." And, while the United States may be the world leader in this sort of research, that's probably not—as critics of universal coverage frequently claim— because of our private insurance system. If anything, it's because of the federal government.

The single biggest source of medical research funding, not just in the United States but in the entire world, is the National Institutes of Health (NIH): Last year, it spent more than $28 billion on research, accounting for about one-third of the total dollars spent on medical research and development in this country (and half the money spent at universities). The majority of that money pays for the kind of basic research that might someday unlock cures for killer diseases like Alzheimer's, AIDS, and cancer. No other country has an institution that matches the NIH in scale. And that is probably the primary explanation for why so many of the intellectual breakthroughs in medical science happen here.

There's no reason why this has to change under universal health insurance. NIH has its own independent funding stream. And, during the late 1990s, thanks to bipartisan agreement between President Clinton and the Republican Congress, its funding actually increased substantially—giving a tremendous boost to research. With or without universal coverage, subsequent presidents and Congress could ramp up funding again—although, if they did so, they would be breaking with the present course. It so happens that, starting in 2003, President Bush and his congressional allies let NIH funding stagnate, even though the cost of medical research (like the cost of medicine overall) was increasing faster than inflation. The reason? They needed room in the budget for other priorities, like tax cuts for the wealthy. In this sense, the greatest threat to future medical breakthroughs may not be universal health care but the people who are trying so hard to fight it.

Periodical Bibliography

The following articles have been selected to supplement the diverse views presented in this chapter.

Clayton M.
Christensen and
Jason Hwang

"Lessons for Obama's Health Care Team," *BusinessWeek*, January 23, 2009.

Dallas Morning News

"Experts Share Views on Health Care Issues," *Dallas Morning News*, May 16, 2009.

David Goldstein

"Q&A: What Health Care Legislation Could Mean for Everyone," *Detroit Free Press*, May 17, 2009.

Jacob S. Hacker

"Healing Our Sicko Health Care System," *New England Journal of Medicine*, January 1, 2009.

Gary Lapon

"Why Women Need Single Payer," *Socialist Worker Online*, May 18, 2009.

*Managed Care
Weekly Digest*

"Health Plans Offer Comprehensive Reform Proposal," December 15, 2008.

Robert O'Harrow, Jr.

"The Machinery Behind Health-Care Reform: How an Industry Lobby Scored a Swift, Unexpected Victory by Channeling Billions to Electronic Health Records," *Washington Post*, May 16, 2009.

Richard Parker

"The 'Federal Health Board,' Another Scheme to Ration Healthcare," *Capitalism Magazine*, January 6, 2009.

Robert Pear

"Health Plans Would Add to Controls on Insurers," *New York Times*, May 15, 2009.

*San Francisco
Chronicle*

"The Year for Health Care," May 17, 2009.

Roger Stark

"Obama's Proposal Is the Non-Competition Health Plan," *Seattle Times*, May 18, 2009.

For Further Discussion

Chapter 1: Is the U.S. Health Care System Failing?

1. Several authors represented in this chapter feel that the U.S. health care system is doing some things very well. List three strengths of the U.S. health care system that are mentioned.

2. Authors of other viewpoints feel that the present system of paying for health care is a burden on the economy, on businesses, and on families. What are some of the facts they cite in support of their views?

3. Do you think that universal access to health care is a necessary or an important goal for the United States to achieve? Why?

Chapter 2: Is Access to Health Care a Moral Issue?

1. Some authors represented in this chapter believe it is immoral to treat access to health care as a human right. Why do they take this position?

2. What role do you think religious beliefs should play in the discussion of health care reform?

3. Several authors write from a religious perspective in support of universal access to health care. What are some of the arguments they use to support their positions?

4. Do you believe that access to health care is a human right? Why or why not?

Chapter 3: Does Universal Health Care Work in Other Countries?

1. How do you explain the fact that the United States is the only modern industrialized country that does not provide

universal access to health care for its citizens? Do you think this is a significant fact?

2. How does the British health care system differ from that in the United States?

3. Which do you think is a better measure of the quality of health care a nation provides, access to childhood immunizations or cancer survival rates?

Chapter 4: What Steps Can the U.S. Take to Achieve Universal Health Care?

1. Several authors discuss Medicare, as either a positive or a negative example of how the health care system could be reformed. Do you think the history of Medicare makes it a good model for a comprehensive universal health care system in the United States? Why or why not?

2. Based on your reading of this chapter, what do you think will be the greatest challenges the United States will face if it does choose to establish a system of universal access to health care?

Organizations to Contact

The editors have compiled the following list of organizations concerned with the issues debated in this book. The descriptions are derived from materials provided by the organizations. All have publications or information available for interested readers. The list was compiled on the date of publication of the present volume; the information provided here may change. Be aware that many organizations take several weeks or longer to respond to inquiries, so allow as much time as possible.

American Association of Retired Persons (AARP)
601 E Street NW, Washington, DC   20049
(800) 424-3410
Web site: www.aarp.org

AARP is a nonprofit, nonpartisan membership organization for people age 50 and older. It provides information and re-sources; advocates on legislative, consumer, and legal issues; assists members to serve their communities; and offers a wide range of unique benefits, special products, and services for members. These benefits include *AARP The Magazine*, the monthly *AARP Bulletin*, and the Spanish-language newspaper, *AARP Segunda Juventud*. The organization is active in every state, the District of Columbia, Puerto Rico, and the U.S. Virgin Islands.

American Enterprise Institute (AEI)
1150 17th Street NW, Washington, DC   20036
(202) 862-5800 • fax: (202) 862-7177
Web site: www.aei.org

The American Enterprise Institute for Public Policy Research is dedicated to preserving and strengthening the foundations of freedom—limited government, private enterprise, vital cul-tural and political institutions, and a strong foreign policy and national defense—through scholarly research, open debate, and publications. Founded in 1943, AEI researches economics and trade; social welfare and health; government tax, spending, regulatory, and legal policies; U.S. politics; international affairs; and U.S. defense and foreign policies. The institute publishes dozens of books and hundreds of articles and reports each year, plus a bimonthly policy magazine, the *American*.

American Medical Association (AMA)

515 N. State Street, Chicago, IL 60654
(800) 621-8335
Web site: www.ama-assn.org

The mission of the AMA is to promote the art and science of medicine and the betterment of public health through core values of leadership, excellence, integrity, and ethical behavior. The AMA has a democratic policy-making process, through which it addresses issues in health care and public policy. Among its many publications are patient education materials and *JAMA* (the *Journal of the American Medical Association*).

American Medical Students Association (AMSA)

1902 Association Drive, Reston, VA 20191
(703) 620-6600 • fax: (703) 620-5873
e-mail: amsa@amsa.org
Web site: www.amsa.org

The American Medical Students Association represents 62,000 medical students, premedical students, interns, residents, and practicing physicians. AMSA is committed to improving health care and health care delivery to all people; promoting active improvement in medical education; involving its members in the social, moral, and ethical obligations of the profession of medicine; assisting in the improvement and understanding of world health problems; contributing to the welfare of medical students, premedical students, interns, residents, and post-MD/DO trainees; and advancing the profession of medicine. AMSA publishes a newsletter and a magazine, the *New Physician*.

American Society of Law, Medicine and Ethics (ASLME)
765 Commonwealth Ave., Suite 1634, Boston, MA   02215
(617) 262-4990 • fax: (617) 437-7596
e-mail: info@aslme.org
Web site: www.aslme.org

The mission of ASLME is to provide high-quality scholarship, debate, and critical thought to professionals in the fields of law, health care, policy, and ethics. The society acts as a source of guidance and information through the publication of two quarterlies, the *Journal of Law, Medicine and Ethics* and the *American Journal of Law and Medicine.*

Brookings Institution
1775 Massachusetts Ave. NW, Washington, DC   20036-2188
(202) 797-6105 • fax: (202) 797-2495
Web site: www.brookings.edu

Founded in 1927, the institution is a liberal research and education organization that publishes material on economics, government, and foreign policy. It strives to serve as a bridge between scholarship and public policy, bringing new knowledge to the attention of decision makers and providing scholars with improved insight into public policy issues. The Brookings Institution produces hundreds of abstracts and reports on health care, with topics ranging from Medicaid to people with disabilities.

Cato Institute
1000 Massachusetts Ave. NW, Washington, DC   20001-5403
(202) 842-0200 • fax: (202) 842-3490
e-mail: cato@cato.org
Web site: www.cato.org

The institute is a libertarian public policy research foundation dedicated to limiting the role of government and protecting individual liberties. Its Health and Welfare Studies department works to formulate and popularize a free-market agenda for health care reform. The institute publishes the quarterly magazine *Regulation*, the bimonthly *Cato Policy Report*, and numerous books and commentaries, hundreds of which relate to health care.

Center for Studying Health System Change (HSC)

600 Maryland Ave. SW, #550, Washington, DC 20024
(202) 484-5261 • fax: (202) 484-9258
Web site: www.hschange.com

The Center for Studying Health System Change is a nonpartisan policy research organization. HSC designs and conducts studies focused on the U.S. health care system to inform the thinking and decisions of policy makers in government and private industry. In addition to this applied use, HSC studies contribute more broadly to the body of health care policy research that enables decision makers to understand changes to the health care system and the national and local market forces driving those changes. It publishes issue briefs, community reports, tracking reports, data bulletins, and journal articles based on its research.

Commonwealth Fund

1 E. 75th Street, New York, NY 10021
(212) 606-3800 • fax: (212) 606-3500
e-mail: info@cmwf.org
Web site: www.cmwf.org

The Commonwealth Fund is a private foundation that aims to promote a high-performing health care system that achieves better access, improved quality, and greater efficiency, particularly for society's most vulnerable, including low-income people, the uninsured, minority Americans, young children, and elderly adults. The fund carries out this mandate by supporting independent research on health care issues and making grants to improve health care practice and policy. An international program in health policy is designed to stimulate innovative policies and practices in the United States and other industrialized countries. The Commonwealth Fund produces more than one hundred publications annually, all free of charge.

Consumers Union, Washington, DC, Office

1101 17th Street NW, Washington, DC   20036
(202) 462-6262 • fax: (202) 265-9548
Web site: www.consumersunion.org

Consumers Union (CU) is a nonprofit organization whose mission is to work for a fair, just, and safe marketplace for all consumers and to empower consumers to protect themselves. CU publishes *Consumer Reports,* one of the top-ten-circulation magazines in the country, and *ConsumerReports.org,* which has the most subscribers of any Web site of its kind. CU also publishes a newsletter, *Consumer Reports on Health,* and maintains a Web site, *PrescriptionforChange.org,* which gathers real-life health care stories that it says it will take to political leaders— including the President, Congress, state lawmakers, and regulators.

Healthcare Leadership Council (HLC)

1001 Pennsylvania Ave. NW, Suite 550 South
Washington, DC   20004
(202) 452-8700 • fax (202) 296-9561
Web site: www.hlc.org

The council is a forum in which health care industry leaders can jointly develop policies, plans, and programs that support a market-based health care system. HLC believes America's health care system should value innovation and provide affordable high-quality health care free from excessive government regulations. It offers the latest press releases on health issues, several public policy papers, and *HLC Healthcare News and Information,* which includes such articles as "Foreign Health Systems Show U.S. What Not to Do" and "Concerns Voiced on Health Reform Measures."

Heritage Foundation

214 Massachusetts Ave. NE, Washington, DC   20002-4999
(202) 546-4400 • fax: (202) 546-8328
e-mail: info@heritage.org
Web site: www.heritage.org

The foundation is a public policy research institute that advocates limited government and the free-market system. It believes the private sector, not government, should be relied upon to ease social problems. The Heritage Foundation publishes hundreds of monographs, books, and background papers with titles such as "The Public Health Insurance Option: Unfair Competition on a Tilting Field" and "Health Care Reform in West Virginia: A Lesson from the States."

Hoover Institution

Stanford University, Stanford, CA   94305-6010
(650) 723-1754 • fax: (650) 723-1687
e-mail: Imaune@stanford.edu
Web site: www.hoover.org

The Hoover Institution on War, Revolution and Peace, Stanford University, is a public policy research center devoted to advanced study of politics, economics, and political economy—both domestic and foreign—as well as international affairs. With its world-renowned group of scholars and ongoing programs of policy-oriented research, the Hoover Institution puts its accumulated knowledge to work as a prominent contributor to the world marketplace of ideas defining a free society. The institution produces numerous books, essays, articles, and journals, including the bimonthly *Policy Review* and quarterly *Hoover Digest*.

Institute for Health Freedom (IHF)

1875 I Street NW, Suite 500, Washington, DC   20006
(202) 429-6610 • fax: (202) 861-1973
e-mail: Feedback@forhealthfreedom.org
Web site: www.forhealthfreedom.org

The institute is a nonpartisan, nonprofit research center established to bring the issues of personal freedom in choosing health care to the forefront of America's health policy debate. Its mission is to present the ethical and economic case for strengthening personal health freedom. IHF publishes *Health Freedom Watch*, a monthly e-newsletter, to alert the public to regulations and policies that affect individuals' right to make free choices about health care.

Institute of Medicine

500 5th Street NW, Washington, DC   20001
(202) 334-2352 • fax: (202) 334-1412
e-mail: iomwww@nas.edu
Web site: www.iom.edu

The Institute of Medicine serves as adviser to the nation to improve health. Established in 1970 under the charter of the National Academy of Sciences, the Institute of Medicine provides independent, objective, evidence-based advice to policy-makers, health professionals, the private sector, and the public. Many of its studies are available online at its Web site. The *IOM News*, a free monthly e-newsletter, is also available.

Henry J. Kaiser Family Foundation (KFF)

2400 Sand Hill Road, Menlo Park, CA   94025
(650) 854-9400 • fax: (650) 854-4800
Web site: www.kff.org

The Henry J. Kaiser Family Foundation is a nonprofit, privately operating foundation focusing on the major health care issues facing the nation. The foundation is an independent voice and source of facts and analysis for policy-makers, the media, the health care community, and the general public. KFF develops and runs its own research and communications programs, often in partnership with outside organizations. The foundation produces policy briefs, studies, fact sheets, reports, and surveys such as "Health Care and the Middle Class: More Costs and Less Coverage" and "Rising Unemployment, Medicaid and the Uninsured."

National Center for Policy Analysis (NCPA)

601 Pennsylvania Ave. NW, Suite 900, South Building
Washington, DC 20004
(202) 220-3082 • fax: (202) 220-3096
e-mail: publications@ncpa.org
Web site: www.ncpa.org

NCPA is a nonprofit public policy research institute. It publishes the weekly *Health Policy Digest* as well as numerous health care policy studies, including "Exposing the Myths of Universal Health Coverage" and "A Framework for Medicare Reform." Its Web site includes an extensive section on health care issues.

National Coalition on Health Care (NCHC)

1200 G Street NW, Suite 810, Washington, DC 20005
(202) 638-7151 • fax: (202) 638-7166
e-mail: info@nchc.org
Web site: www.nchc.org

NCHC is a nonprofit, nonpartisan group that represents the nation's largest alliance working to improve America's health care and make it more affordable. The coalition offers several policy studies, including *Building a Better Health Care System: Specifications for Reform* and *Prevention's Potential for Slowing the Growth of Medical Spending*.

National Medical Association (NMA)

1012 10th Street NW, Washington, DC 20001
(202) 347-1895 • fax: (202) 898-2510
e-mail: HealthPolicy@nmanet.org
Web site: www.nmanet.org

The National Medical Association (NMA) is the collective voice of African American physicians and the leading force for parity and justice in medicine and the elimination of disparities in health. NMA is the largest and oldest national organization representing African American physicians and their patients in the United States. Throughout its history the NMA has focused primarily on health issues related to African Americans and medically underserved populations; its principles, goals, initiatives, and philosophy encompass all ethnic groups, however. It publishes the monthly *Journal of the National Medical Association*.

Physicians for a National Health Program (PNHP)

29 E. Madison, Suite 602, Chicago, IL   60602
(312) 782-6006 • fax: (312) 782-6007
e-mail: info@pnhp.org
Web site: www.pnhp.org

PNHP is a single-issue organization advocating a universal, comprehensive single-payer national health program. Its members and physician activists organize rallies, town hall meetings, and debates; coordinate speakers and forum discussions; contribute op-eds and articles to the nation's top newspapers, medical journals, and magazines; and appear regularly on national television and news programs advocating for a single-payer system. Its Web site features a blog.

The Robert Wood Johnson Foundation

P.O. Box 2316, Princeton, NJ   08543
(877) 843-7953
Web site: www.rwjf.org/

The Robert Wood Johnson Foundation is an independent philanthropic organization devoted to improving health policy and practice. It works with a diverse group of people and organizations to improve health care delivery and to help make a difference on the widest scale. Projects funded by the Robert Wood Johnson Foundation fall into one of seven program areas: human-capital building, childhood obesity, expansion of health care coverage, innovative practices, public health, quality health care for all, and vulnerable populations. Resources on health reform can be found on its Web site.

Single Payer Action

P.O. Box 18384, Washington, DC   20036
e-mail: action@singlepayeraction.org
Web site: www. singlepayeraction.org

Single Payer Action is a national nonprofit organization that is committed to implementing a single-payer health insurance system—"Medicare for all"—in the United States. Single Payer Action organizes events that bring health care activists face-to-face with the health insurance industry and legislators. A list of resources can be found on its Web site.

Urban Institute

2100 M Street NW, Washington, DC   20037
(202) 833-7200
Web site: www.urban.org

The Urban Institute investigates social and economic problems confronting the nation and analyzes efforts to solve these problems. It also works to improve government decisions and to increase citizens' awareness about important public choices. It offers a wide variety of resources, including books and reports such as *Making a Business Case for Reducing Racial and Ethnic Disparities in Health Care* and *How We Can Pay for Health Reform.*

Bibliography of Books

Henry J. Aaron and Lindsay M. James
Agenda for the Nation. Washington, DC: Brookings Institution Press, 2003.

Ron Angel, Laura Lein, and Jane Henrici
Poor Families in America's Health Care Crisis. New York: Cambridge University Press, 2006.

Daniel Brook
The Trap: Selling Out to Stay Afloat in Winner-Take-All America. New York: Times Books, 2007.

Daniel Callahan and Angela A. Wasunna
Medicine and the Market: Equity v. Choice. Baltimore: Johns Hopkins University Press, 2006.

James Carville
Had Enough? A Handbook for Fighting Back. New York: Simon & Schuster, 2003.

Christine K. Cassel
Medicare Matters: What Geriatric Medicine Can Teach American Health Care. New York: University of California Press, 2005.

Jonathan Cohn
Sick: The Untold Story of America's Health Care Crisis—And the People Who Pay the Price. New York: HarperCollins, 2007.

David M. Cutler
Your Money or Your Life: Strong Medicine for America's Health Care System. New York: Oxford University Press, 2004.

Sheldon Danziger and Daniel H. Weinberg — *Fighting Poverty: What Works and What Doesn't*. Cambridge MA: Harvard University Press, 1986.

Thomas Daschle, Scott S. Greenberger, and Jeanne M. Lambrew — *Critical: What We Can Do About the Health-Care Crisis*. New York: Thomas Dunne Books, 2008.

Alan Derickson — *Health Security for All: Dreams of Universal Health Care in America*. Baltimore: Johns Hopkins University Press, 2005.

Lou Dobbs — *War on the Middle Class: How the Government, Big Business, and Special Interest Groups Are Waging War on the American Dream and How to Fight Back*. New York: Viking Press, 2006.

Barbara Ehrenreich — *This Land Is Their Land: Reports from a Divided Nation*. New York: Metropolitan Books, 2008.

Larry Elder — *The Ten Things You Can't Say in America*. New York: St. Martin's Press, 2000.

Ezekiel Emanuel — *Healthcare, Guaranteed: A Simple, Secure Solution for America*. New York: Public Affairs, 2008.

Rahm Emanuel — *The Plan: Big Ideas for Change in America*. New York: Public Affairs, 2006.

Kenneth A. Fisher, Lindsay E. Rockwell, and Missy Scott — *In Defiance of Death: Exposing the Real Costs of End-of-Life Care.* Westport, CT: Praeger, 2008.

Jason Furman — *Who Has the Cure? Hamilton Project Ideas on Health Care.* Washington, DC: Brookings Institution, 2008.

John C. Goodman, Gerald L. Musgrave, and Devon M. Herrick — *Lives at Risk: Single-Payer National Health Insurance Around the World.* Lanham, MD: Rowman & Littlefield, 2004.

Colin Gordon — *Dead on Arrival: The Politics of Health Care in America.* Princeton, NJ: Princeton University Press, 2003.

Jacob S. Hacker — *The Great Risk Shift: The Assault on American Jobs, Families, Health Care and Retirement, and How You Can Fight Back.* New York: Oxford University Press, 2006.

George C. Halvorson — *Health Care Reform Now! A Prescription for Change.* San Francisco: Jossey-Bass, 2007.

Lisa I. Iezzoni and Bonnie O'Day — *More Than Ramps: A Guide to Improving Health Quality and Access for People with Disabilities.* New York: Oxford University Press, 2006.

Institute of Medicine — *Crossing the Quality Chasm: A New Health System for the 21st Century.* Washington, DC: National Academy Press, 2001.

Michael B. Katz — *The Price of Citizenship: Redefining the American Welfare State.* New York: Metropolitan Books, 2001.

Laurence J. Kotlikoff — *The Healthcare Fix: Universal Insurance for All Americans.* Cambridge, MA: MIT Press, 2007.

Robert H. LeBow — *Health Care Meltdown: Confronting the Myths and Fixing Our Failing System.* Chambersburg, PA: A.C. Hood, 2003.

Roice D. Luke, Stephen Lee, and Patrick Michael Plummer — *Healthcare Strategy in Pursuit of Competitive Advantage.* Chicago: Health Administration Press, 2004.

George D. Lundberg and James Stacey — *Severed Trust: Why American Medicine Hasn't Been Fixed.* New York: Basic Books, 2000.

David Mechanic — *The Truth About Health Care: Why Reform Is Not Working in America.* New Brunswick, NJ: Rutgers University Press, 2006.

Steven A. Nyce and Sylvester J. Schieber — *The Economic Implications of Aging Societies: The Costs of Living Happily Ever After.* New York: Cambridge University Press, 2005.

Sally Pipes — *Miracle Cure: How to Solve America's Health Care Crisis and Why Canada Isn't the Answer,* San Francisco: Pacific Research Institute, 2004.

Jill S. Quadagno   *One Nation, Uninsured: Why the U.S.*
                        Has No National Health Insurance.
                        New York: Oxford University Press,
                        2005.

Arnold S. Relman   *A Second Opinion: Rescuing America's*
                        Healthcare: A Plan for Universal
                        Coverage Serving Patients Over Profit.
                        New York: Public Affairs, 2007.

Julius B.   *The Health Care Mess: How We Got*
Richmond and   *Into It, and What It Will Take to Get*
Rashi Fein   *Out.* Cambridge, MA: Harvard
                        University Press, 2005.

Susan Starr Sered   *Uninsured in America: Life and Death*
and Rushika J.   *in the Land of Opportunity.* Berkeley,
Fernandopulle   CA: University of California Press,
                        2005.

Rachel E. Spector   *Cultural Diversity in Health and*
                        Illness. Saddle River, NJ: Pearson
                        Prentice Hall, 2004.

Ken Terry   *Rx for Health Care Reform.* Nashville,
                        TN: Vanderbilt University Press,
                        2007.

Robert M. Veatch   *Patient, Heal Thyself: How the New*
                        Medicine Puts the Patient in Charge.
                        New York: Oxford University Press,
                        2009.

Index